SUMMER MATH WORKBOOK

Bridge Building Activities

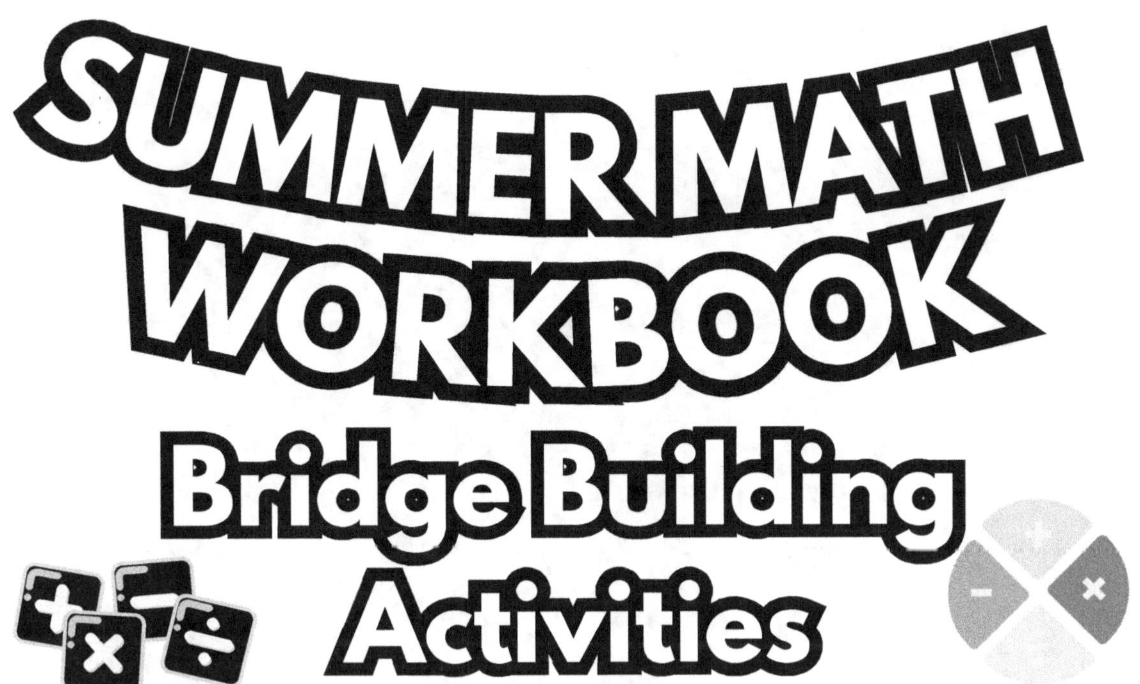

Introduction

As parents and educators, we understand the pivotal role that mathematics plays in shaping a child's academic journey and future success. Yet, the path to mathematical proficiency can often seem daunting, filled with challenges and complexities. That's where the transformative power of Summer Bridge Building Activities books comes into play, illuminating the way forward with clarity, precision, and purpose.

Summer vacation is a time for rest and relaxation, but it also presents the risk of the "summer slide," where students lose some of the academic gains they made during the school year. Summer Bridge Building Activities books are specifically designed to tackle this challenge, ensuring that your child stays academically engaged and prepared for the upcoming school year. These books provide a seamless bridge from one grade to the next, reinforcing essential skills and introducing new concepts that will give your child a head start.

Imagine your child eagerly diving into the pages of a Summer Bridge Building Activities book, greeted by clear, engaging content that demystifies complex mathematical concepts. With each turn of the pages, they embark on a journey of discovery, encountering thoughtfully curated practice questions that reinforce learning and sharpen problem-solving skills. As they unveil the answers to those questions, a sense of accomplishment blossoms within them — a tangible reward for their hard work and dedication.

Summer Bridge Building Activities books transcend traditional educational tools; they are meticulously crafted to build a deep and enduring understanding of mathematics. These books follow a sequential and logical progression, starting from fundamental principles and advancing to sophisticated problem-solving strategies. Each chapter is designed to build on the previous one, ensuring a solid and comprehensive foundation for future learning.

Parents, we yearn for nothing more than to see our children thrive academically and personally. We want to witness the spark of inspiration ignited within them as they overcome academic challenges with confidence and poise. Summer Bridge Building Activities books serve as indispensable partners in this noble endeavor, offering not just practice questions but the keys to unlocking a world of academic and personal opportunities.

Visualize the pride on your child's face as they master a challenging math concept, the joy they experience when their efforts yield results, and the confidence they gain with each success. These pages are designed to make learning math a positive, enriching, and deeply rewarding experience that will benefit them throughout their academic journey and beyond.

For educators, Summer Bridge Building Activities books are invaluable allies in the quest to cultivate mathematical proficiency in the classroom. Accompanied by comprehensive guides and readily available answers, instructors can focus on mentoring and nurturing their students, secure in the knowledge that these books provide a robust framework for effective learning.

Within the pages of Summer Bridge Building Activities books lies not just the promise of academic excellence, but the seeds of a brighter future. By integrating these resources into your child's summer routine, you are bestowing upon them the gifts of confidence, curiosity, and a lifelong love of learning.

Invest in your child's future today with Summer Bridge Building Activities books — because every great journey begins with a single step, and this step can change everything. Keep the momentum of learning alive over the summer, and watch your child soar to new academic heights.

Contents

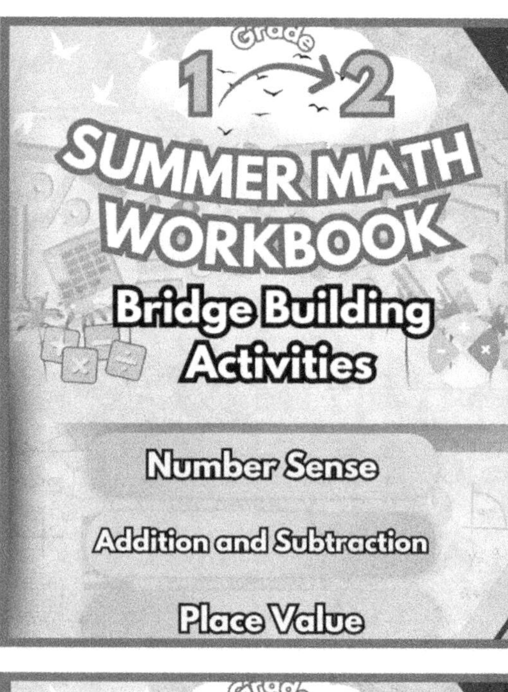
Grade
1 → 2
SUMMER MATH
WORKBOOK
Bridge Building
Activities
Number Sense
Addition and Subtraction
Place Value

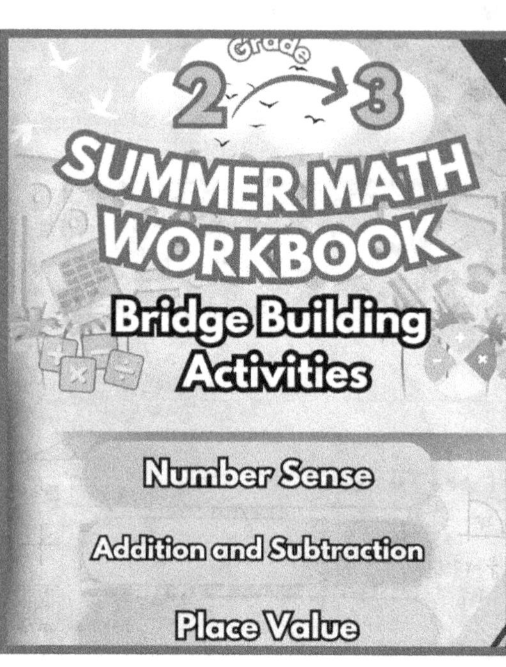
Grade
2 → 3
SUMMER MATH
WORKBOOK
Bridge Building
Activities
Number Sense
Addition and Subtraction
Place Value

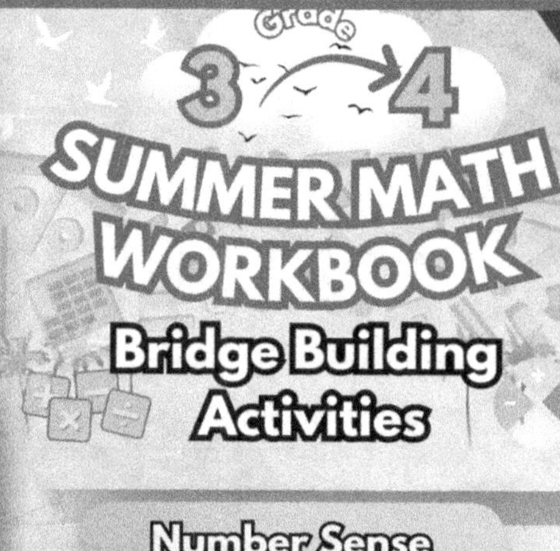
Grade
3 → 4
SUMMER MATH
WORKBOOK
Bridge Building
Activities
Number Sense
Addition and Subtraction
Place Value

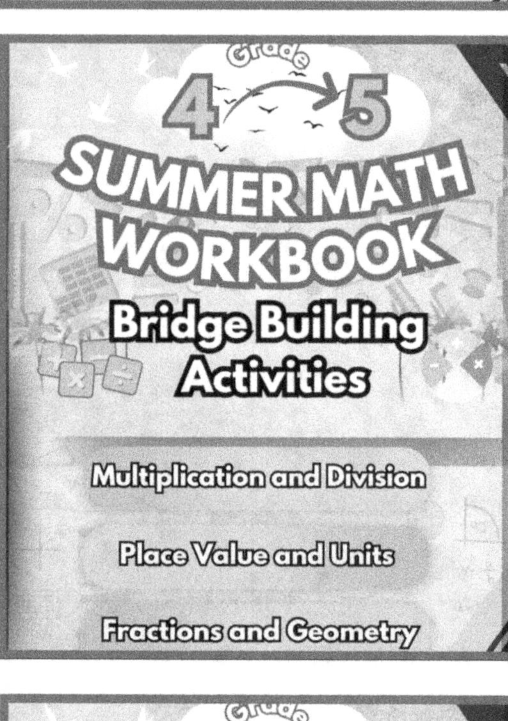
Grade
4 → 5
SUMMER MATH
WORKBOOK
Bridge Building
Activities
Multiplication and Division
Place Value and Units
Fractions and Geometry

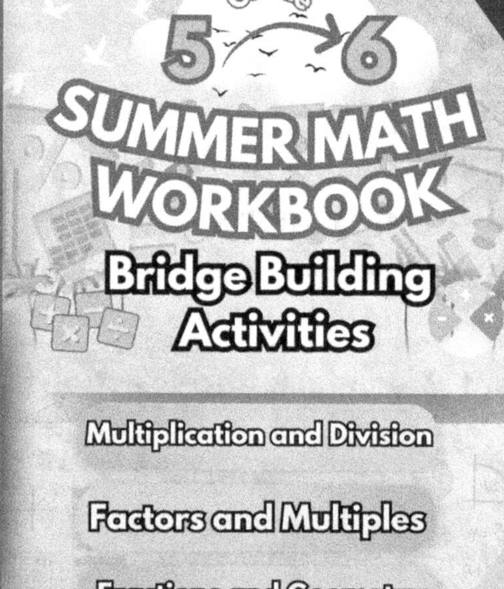
Grade
5 → 6
SUMMER MATH
WORKBOOK
Bridge Building
Activities
Multiplication and Division
Factors and Multiples
Fractions and Geometry

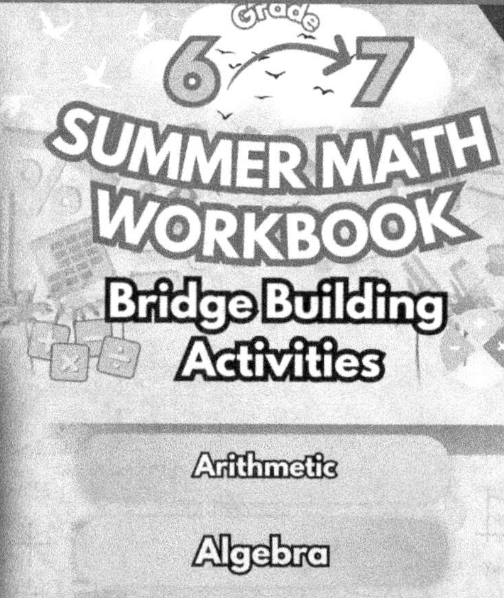
Grade
6 → 7
SUMMER MATH
WORKBOOK
Bridge Building
Activities
Arithmetic
Algebra
Geometry and Statistics

Grade
7 → 8
SUMMER MATH
WORKBOOK
Bridge Building
Activities
Ratio and Percentage
Algebra and Cartesian Plane
Geometry and Statistics

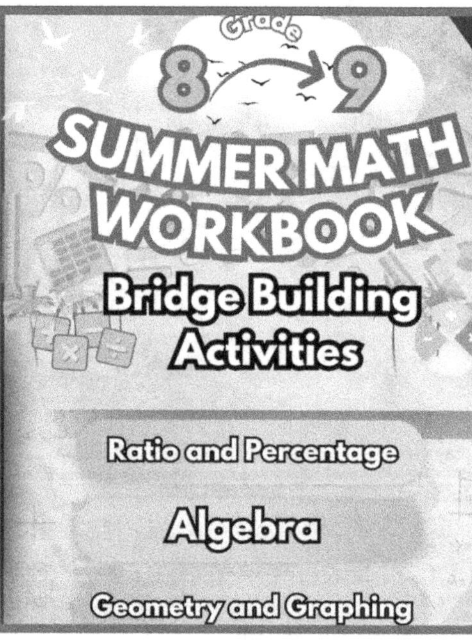
Grade
8 → 9
SUMMER MATH
WORKBOOK
Bridge Building
Activities
Ratio and Percentage
Algebra
Geometry and Graphing

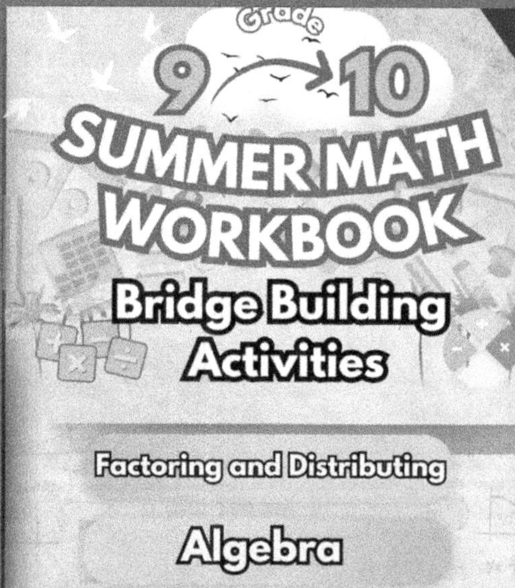
Grade
9 → 10
SUMMER MATH
WORKBOOK
Bridge Building
Activities
Factoring and Distributing
Algebra
Geometry and Graphing

<u>Pre-Algebra</u>

<u>Simplifying expressions</u>

It involves combining like terms and performing operations to make the expression easier to understand and work with.

Let's simplify the expression:

$$2x - 2x + 8 + 4$$

- **Combine like terms:** First, we look for terms with the same variable and exponent. In this expression, $2x$ and $-2x$ are like terms, so they can be combined:

$$2x - 2x = 0$$

- **Substitute the simplified terms:** After combining the like terms, the expression becomes:

$$0 + 8 + 4$$

- **Combine the remaining terms:** Now, we add the constants together:

$$8 + 4 = 12$$

<u>Order of Operations (PEMDAS)</u>

The order of operations, often remembered by the acronym PEMDAS, stands for:

- **Parentheses**: Perform operations inside parentheses first.

- **Exponents**: Evaluate exponents (powers and roots) next.

- **Multiplication and Division**: Perform multiplication and division from left to right.

- **Addition and Subtraction:** Perform addition and subtraction from left to right.

The order of operations helps to clarify which operations should be performed first in a mathematical expression to ensure consistent and accurate results.

- **Parentheses**: Evaluate expressions within parentheses first. If there are nested parentheses, start with the innermost ones and work your way out.

    1. Example: $2 \times (3 + 4) = 2 \times 7 = 14$

- **Exponents**: Evaluate expressions with exponents (powers and roots) next.

    1. Example: $2^3 + 4 = 8 + 4 = 12$

- **Multiplication and Division**: Perform multiplication and division from left to right.

    1. Example: $2 \times 3 + 4 = 6 + 4 = 10$

    2. Example: $6 \div 2 \times 3 = 3 \times 3 = 9$

- **Addition and Subtraction**: Perform addition and subtraction from left to right.

    1. Example: 2 + 3 × 4 = 2 + 12 =14

    2. Example: 10 − 4 ÷ 2 = 10 − 2 = 8

Simplify Equations

Evaluating expressions involves substituting given values for variables in an expression and then performing the indicated operations to find the result.

For example: Let's evaluate 4x − 10, when x = 3:

Step 1: Substitute the given value for the variable:

Replace every occurrence of x in the expression 4x − 10 with the given value, which is 3:

$$= 4(3) − 10$$

Step 2: Perform the operations:

Perform the indicated operations according to the order of operations (PEMDAS - Parentheses, Exponents, Multiplication and Division, Addition and Subtraction):

$$= 4 × 3 − 10$$

Step 3: Simplify:

Calculate the result:

$$12 - 10 = 2$$

Solving Inequalities

Inequalities are mathematical expressions that compare the relative sizes of two values. They are used to express relationships where one quantity is:

- $"<"$ (less than),
- $">"$ (greater than),
- $"<="$ (less than or equal to),
- $">="$ (greater than or equal to),
- and $"\neq"$ (not equal to) another quantity.

For example:

$$y + -10 \leq -8$$

To isolate y, we need to get rid of the constant term -10. Since -10 is being subtracted from y, we can undo this operation by adding 10 to both sides of the inequality:

$$y - 10 + 10 \leq -8 + 10$$

$$y \leq 2$$

To check the solution:

$$2 - 10 \leq -8$$

$$-8 = -8$$

The inequality is true when $y = 2$

Verbal Algebra Expressions

Verbal algebra involves translating word problems or verbal statements into algebraic expressions or equations.

For example: The product of the two numbers is 91. One number is six less than the other. What are the numbers?

We're given a verbal description of a problem, and we need to represent it using algebraic symbols and equations.

Let's break down the given problem into algebraic expressions:

- Given that the product of the two numbers is 91, we can write the equation: $xy = 91$
- Also, given that one number is six less than the other, we can write another equation: $x = y - 6$

Now, we can use algebraic techniques to solve the system of equations to find the values of x and y, which represent the two numbers.

$$x(x - 6) = 91$$

1. **Solve the equation:**

   - Expand the equation:

   $$x^2 - 6x = 91$$

   - Rearrange the equation into standard quadratic form:

   $$x^2 - 6x - 91 = 0$$

   - Factor the quadratic equation:

   $$(x - 13)(x + 7) = 0$$

2. **Find the solutions for x:**

   - From the factored form, we have two possible values for x:

   $$x = 13 \text{ or } x = -7$$

3. **Check the validity of the solutions:**

   - Since one number is six less than the other, we discard the negative solution.

   - Therefore, the solution is $x = 13$.

4. **Find the other number:**

   - Substitute $x = 13$ into the expression for the other number:

Other number $= x - 6 = 13 - 6 = 7$

So, the two numbers are 13 and 7.

Solving Equations (One Side)

Solving one-step equations involves performing a single operation to isolate the variable and find its value.

Let's solve an equation step by step: $16 + x = 31$

1. **Identify the Goal**:

    The goal is to isolate the variable x on one side of the equation.

2. **Simplify the Equation**: Combine like terms on both sides of the equation, if necessary.

    The equation is already simplified.

3. **Undo Addition or Subtraction**: If there's addition or subtraction involving the variable, undo it by performing the opposite operation on both sides of the equation.

    Since x is being added to 16, we'll undo this operation by subtracting 16 from both sides of the equation:

    $$16 + x - 16 = 31 - 16$$

4. **Isolate the Variable**: Ensure that the variable is alone on one side of the equation.

$$X = 15$$

5. **Check Your Solution**: Substitute the value of x back into the original equation to verify that it satisfies the equation.

$$16 + 15 = 31$$

$$31 = 31$$

The equation is balanced, so the solution.

Equations (Two Sides)

A two-sided equation is an equation where both sides have expressions with variables and constants. The goal when solving a two-sided equation is to find the value of the variable that makes both sides equal.

For example: Let's solve an equation:

$$9 + 8x + 8 = 64 + x + 2$$

- **Combine Like Terms:** Simplify each side of the equation by combining like terms (terms with the same variable or constants).

$$9 + 8x + 8 = 64 + x + 2$$

$$17 + 8x = 66 + x$$

- **Isolate the Variable:** Use inverse operations to isolate the variable on one side of the equation.

    subtract x from both sides:

    $$17 + 8x - x = 66 + x - x$$

    $$17 + 7x = 66$$

    subtracting 17 from both sides:

    $$17 - 17 + 7x = 66 - 17$$

    $$7x = 49$$

    divide both sides by 7:

    $$\frac{7x}{7} = \frac{49}{7} = x = 7$$

- **Check Solution:** Once you find the solution, substitute it back into the original equation to ensure it makes the equation true.

    Substitute $x = 7$ back into the original equation:

    $$9 + 8(7) + 8 = 64 + 7 + 2$$

    $$9 + 56 + 8 = 64 + 7 + 2$$

    $$73 = 73$$

Percentage

Percentage is a way of expressing a number as a fraction of 100. It is commonly used to represent proportions, rates, and comparisons. The symbol "%" is used to denote percentages.

To calculate a percentage, we multiply the given number by the appropriate fraction or decimal equivalent.

How to calculate a percentage:

Convert Percentage to Decimal: If the percentage is given as a percentage value (e.g., 25%), convert it to its decimal equivalent by dividing by 100.

$$\text{For example, 25\% as a decimal is } \frac{25}{100} = 0.25$$

Multiply: Multiply the decimal equivalent of the percentage by the given number. This gives us the portion of the number that represents the percentage.

$$100 \times 0.25 = 25\%$$

Result: The result is the calculated percentage value.

For example, to calculate 25% of 80:

Convert 25% to a decimal: 25% = 0.25.

Multiply 0.25 by 80: $0.25 \times 80 = 20$. The result is 20.

<u>Linear Equation</u>

A linear equation is an algebraic equation that represents a straight line when graphed on a coordinate plane. It consists of variables raised to the power of 1 (i.e., no exponents higher than 1) and constant coefficients.

The general form of a linear equation in one variable x is:

$$ax + b = 0$$

Where a and b are constants, and x is the variable.

Let's solve the linear equation:

$$-2x + 9 = 5$$

- **Isolate the variable term:** We want to isolate the term containing x on one side of the equation. To do this, we'll move the constant term to the other side. Subtract 9 from both sides:

$$-2x + 9 - 9 = 5 - 9$$

$$-2x = -4$$

- **Divide by the coefficient of the variable:** To solve for x, divide both sides by the coefficient of x, which is -2:

$$\frac{-2x}{-2} = \frac{-4}{-2}$$

$$x = 2$$

<u>**Slop from Two Points**</u>

The slope between two points on a Cartesian coordinate system is a measure of the steepness of the line connecting those points. It's calculated by finding the change in the y-coordinates divided by the change in the x-coordinates.

- The coordinates of the first point as $(x1, y1) = (2, -30)$.

- The coordinates of the second point as $(x2, y2) = (-5, 40)$.

The formula to calculate the slope (m) between two points:

$$\frac{y2 - y1}{x2 - x1}$$

$$= \frac{40 - (-30)}{-5 - 2} = \frac{70}{-7}$$

Slope =   −10

<u>**Plot Lines**</u>

To plot the lines using the given points, we'll first locate each point on the coordinate plane, and then connect the points to form the lines. Let's plot each line one by one:

A = (-6, -3)   B = (0, 3)

C = (-4, -1)   D = (1, 4)

E = (4, 7)   F = (2, 5)

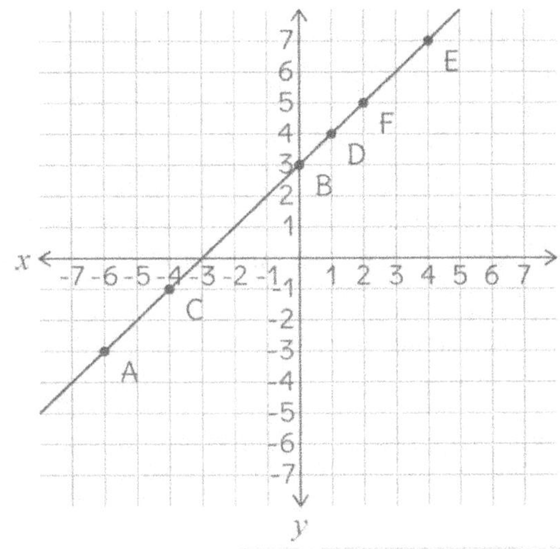

Graphing Linear Equation

Graphing a linear equation involves plotting the points that satisfy the equation on a coordinate plane and connecting them to form a straight line. Linear equations are equations of the form $y = mx + b$, where m represents the slope of the line, and b represents the y-intercept, the point where the line intersects the y-axis.

To graph a linear equation:

1. Identify the slope (m) and y-intercept (b) from the equation.

2. Plot the y-intercept $(0,b)$) as a point on the y-axis.

3. Use the slope to find additional points on the line. The slope represents the change in y for every unit change in x.

4. Connect the points to form a straight line.

For example, to graph the equation:

$$y = \frac{9}{4}x - 8$$

1. **Identify the slope and y-intercept:** The slope is $\frac{9}{4}$, and the y-intercept is −8.

2. **Plot the y-intercept:** Plot the point $(0,-8)$.

3. **Use the slope to plot additional points:** the slop is $\frac{9}{4}$ to find another point. we will move up 9 units and 4 units to the right from the y-intercept to find another point.

4. **Draw the line:** Once we have at least two points, we can draw a straight line.

We can continue this process to plot more points and extend the line further if needed.

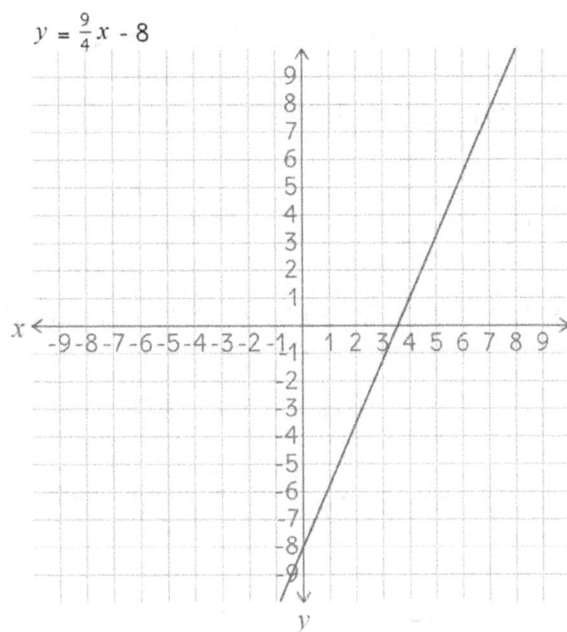

System of Equations

A system of equations is a collection of two or more equations involving the same set of variables. The solution to a system of equations is the set of values for the variables that satisfy all the equations simultaneously.

Solving by Elimination:

To solve a system of equations by elimination, we manipulate the equations to eliminate one of the variables.

Given the system:

$$4x + 5y = 6$$

$$10x + 6y = 8$$

Step 1: Multiply each equation by a constant such that the coefficients of one of the variables become equal or multiples of each other.

Let's try to eliminate the variable x.

- Multiply the first equation by 5 and the second equation by -2:

$$20x + 25y = 30$$

$$-20x - 12y = -16$$

Step 2: Add the two equations together to eliminate the variable x:

$$(20x - 20x) + (25y - 12y) = 30 - 16$$

$$13y = 14$$

$$y = \frac{14}{13} = 1.077$$

Step 3: Solve for y:

Step 4: Substitute the value of y into one of the original equations to solve for x. Let's use the first equation:

$$4x + 5\left(\frac{14}{13}\right) = 6$$

$$4x + \frac{70}{13} = 6$$

$$4x = 6 - \frac{70}{13}$$

$$4x = \frac{78 - 70}{13}$$

$$4x = \frac{8}{13}$$

$$X = \frac{2}{13} = 0.154$$

the solution to the system of equations is x =0.154 and y = 1.077.

Cartesian Plane

Cartesian Coordinates

The Cartesian Coordinate System, also known as the x-y plane, provides a method for representing points on a graph using two perpendicular lines: the x-axis and the y-axis. At their intersection, denoted by the letter "O", lies the origin.

To plot a point on this system, we use coordinates, consisting of two numbers. The first number represents the horizontal movement from the origin (x-coordinate), while the second number represents the vertical movement (y-coordinate). These coordinates are written as an ordered pair (x, y).

For instance, let's plot these coordinates:

$$A = (1, 3) \qquad B = (5, 0) \qquad C = (8, 6)$$

$$D = (9, 5) \qquad E = (1, 9) \qquad F = (3, 1)$$

$$G = (0, 8) \qquad H = (4, 6) \qquad I = (4, 9)$$

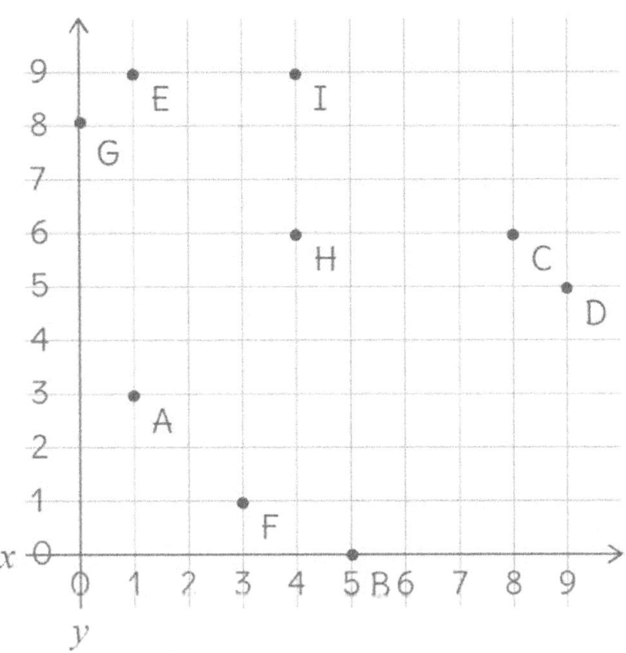

Cartesian Coordinates (Four Quadrants)

In a Cartesian coordinate system with four quadrants, there are two

perpendicular number lines intersecting at the origin (0,0), dividing the plane

into four quadrants.

To plot a point in this Cartesian coordinate system, we use an ordered pair (x,

y), where x represents the distance from the y-axis, and y represents the

distance from the x-axis.

For instance, let's plot these coordinates:

A = (-4, 1)   B = (2, 1)   C = (4, 2)

5
4
3
2
1
C
A
B
x
-5 -4 -3 -2 -1
1 2 3 4 5
-1
-2
-3
-4
-5
y

<u>Geometry</u>

<u>Area and Perimeter</u>

The area of a shape represents the amount of space it occupies. The perimeter of a shape is the total distance around its outer edge.

Area of Rectangle

For a square, since all four sides are equal, we only need to know the length of one side to find its area. We can calculate the area of a square by multiplying the length of one side by itself (squared). So, if the length of one side of the square is 's', then the area (A) is given by:

$A = s \times s$

$A = 4 \times 4$

$A = 16$

Perimeter of Rectangle

For a square, since all four sides are equal, we can find the perimeter by adding up the lengths of all four sides. If 's' represents the length of one side, then the perimeter (P) is given by:

$$P = 4 \times s$$

$$P = 4 \times 4$$

$$P = 16$$

Area of Triangle:

The area of a triangle represents the amount of space enclosed within its three sides. The formula for calculating the area of a triangle depends on the type of triangle. For a general triangle, we use the formula:

$$A = \frac{1}{2} \times \text{base} \times \text{height}$$

Where:

- A represents the area of the triangle.

- The base is the length of any one side of the triangle.

- The height is the perpendicular distance from the base to the opposite vertex.

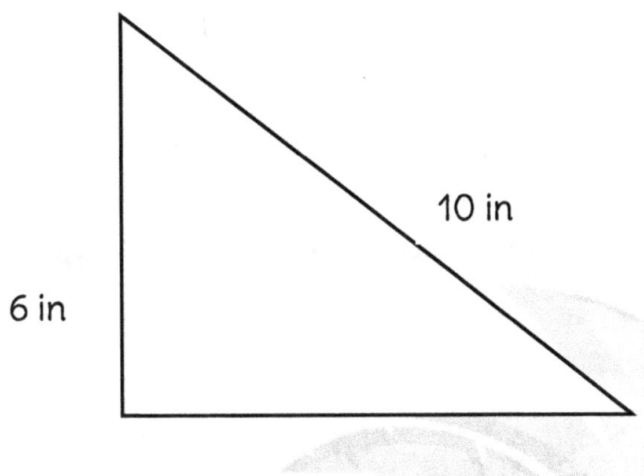

$$A = \frac{1}{2} \times \text{base} \times \text{height}$$

$$A = \frac{1}{2} \times 6 \times 8$$

$$A = \frac{1}{2} \times 48$$

$$A = 24$$

Perimeter of Triangle:

The perimeter of a triangle is the total length of its three sides. To find the perimeter, we simply add the lengths of all three sides together:

$$P = \text{side1} + \text{side2} + \text{side3}$$

$$P = 6 + 8 + 10$$

$$P = 24$$

<u>**Equilateral Triangle**</u>

An equilateral triangle is a triangle in which all three sides are equal in length. To find the area and perimeter of an equilateral triangle, we can use the following formulas:

- Area (A): $\frac{\sqrt{3}}{4} \times a^2$ where a is the length of one side of the equilateral triangle.
- Perimeter (P): $P = 3a$ where a is the length of one side of the equilateral triangle.

Area of Equilateral Triangle:

$$\text{Area (A): } \frac{\sqrt{3}}{4} \times (6)^2$$

$$\text{Area (A): } \frac{\sqrt{3}}{4} \times 36$$

$$\text{Area (A): } \frac{36\sqrt{3}}{4}$$

$$\text{Area (A): } \frac{36(1.73)}{4}$$

$$\text{Area (A): } \frac{62.35}{4}$$

$$\text{Area (A): } 15.59 \text{ in}^2$$

Perimeter of Equilateral Triangle:

$$P = 3a$$

$$P = 3(6) = 18$$

Isosceles Triangle

An isosceles triangle is a triangle with at least two sides of equal length. The angles opposite the equal sides are also equal.

Area of Isosceles Triangle

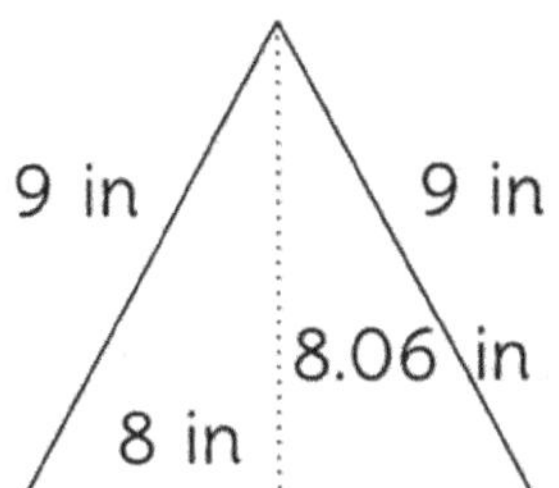

$$A = \frac{1}{2} \times \text{base} \times \text{height}$$

$$A = \frac{1}{2} \times 8 \times 8$$

$$A = \frac{1}{2} \times 64$$

$$A = 32$$

Perimeter of Isosceles Triangle

The perimeter of a triangle is the total length of its three sides. To find the perimeter, we simply add the lengths of all three sides together:

$$P = side1 + side2 + side3$$

$$P = 9 + 9 + 8$$

$$P = 26$$

Scalene Triangle

A scalene triangle is a triangle with no equal sides and no equal angles. The formula for finding various properties of a scalene triangle is as follows:

Area (A): The area of a scalene triangle can be calculated using Heron's fo rmula, which is given by:

$$A = \sqrt{s(s-a)(s-b)(s-c)}$$

where s is the semi-perimeter of the triangle,

and a, b, and c are the lengths of its three sides.

Perimeter (P): The perimeter of a scalene triangle is the sum of the lengths of its three sides.

$$P = side1 + side2 + side3$$

Let's find the Area and Perimeter of a Scalene Triangle:

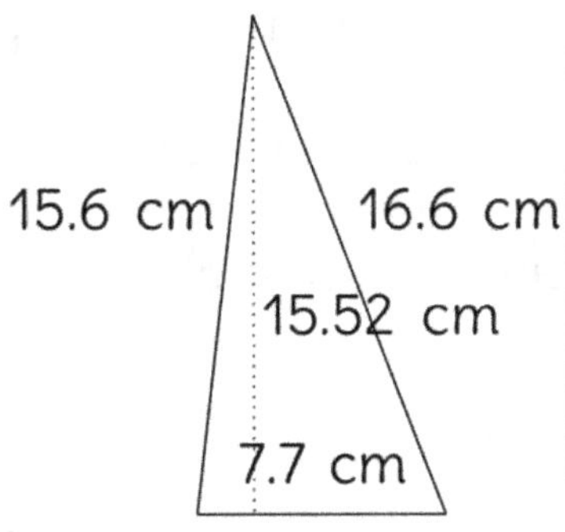

Area (A): First, we calculate the semi-perimeter (s):

$$S = \frac{a + b + c}{2} = \frac{15.6 + 16.6 + 7.7}{2} = \frac{39.8}{2} = 19.9 \text{ cm}$$

Heron's formula to find the area:

$$A = \sqrt{s(s-a)(s-b)(s-c)}$$

$$A = \sqrt{19.9\,(19.9 - 15.6)(19.9 - 16.6)(19.9 - 7.7)}$$

$$A = \sqrt{19.9 \times 4.3 \times 3.3 \times 12.2}$$

$$A = \sqrt{3445} \approx 59$$

Perimeter (P):

$$P = side1 + side2 + side3$$

$$P = 15.6 + 16.6 + 7.7$$

$$P = 39.8$$

Area and Perimeter of an L-shape

The L-shaped figure typically consists of two rectangles joined together to form an L-shape. To find the area and perimeter of an L-shaped figure, we will need to calculate the areas and perimeters of each rectangle and then combine them.

Area=Area of Rectangle 1 + Area of Rectangle 2

Perimeter=Perimeter of Rectangle 1 + Perimeter of Rectangle 2

Let's find the Area and Perimeter of an L-shape:

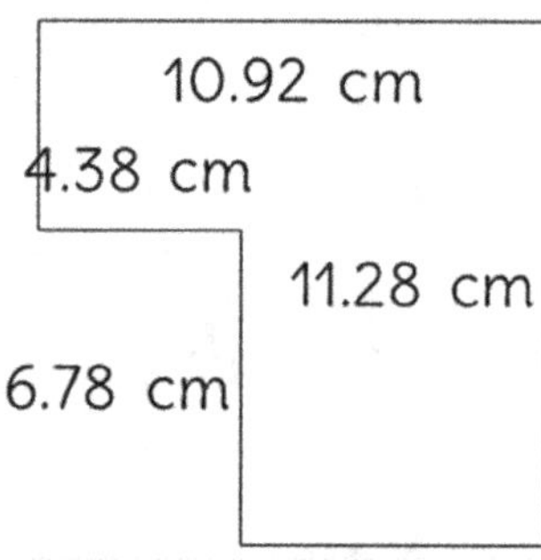

Area of L-Shape

Area 1 = 4.38 x 4.5 = 19.7 cm²

Area 2 = 11.28 x 6.54 = 73.7 cm²

Area = 19.7 + 73.7

Area = 93.481 cm²

Perimeter of L-Shape

$$P = 11.28 + 6.54 + 6.78 + 4.38 + 4.5 + 10.92$$

$$P = 44.4 \text{ cm}$$

Area and Perimeter of U-shape

U-shape is basically composed of three rectangles, we'll need to calculate the area and perimeter of each rectangle separately and then sum them up.

Area of the U-shape:

The total area (A) of the U-shape is the sum of the areas of the three rectangles:

$$A = A1 + A2 + A3$$

Perimeter of the U-shape: The total perimeter (P) of the U-shape is the sum of the perimeters of the three rectangles:

$$P = P1 + P2 + P3$$

Let's find the area and perimeter of the following U-shape:

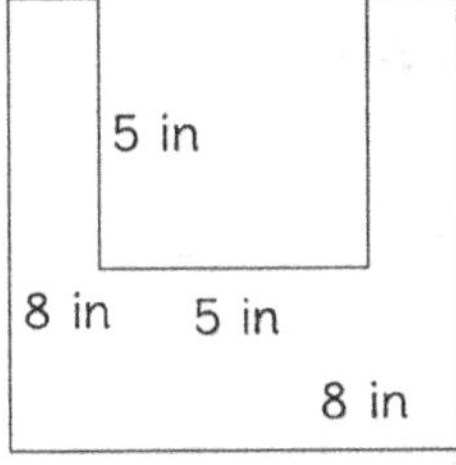

Area:

$$A1 = 8 \times 1.5 = 12 + A2 = 3 \times 5 = 15 + A3 = 8 \times 1.5 = 12$$

$$= 12 + 15 + 12$$

$$= 39 \text{ in}^2$$

Perimeter:

$$2 \times 8 + 2 \times 5 + 2 \times 8$$

$$= 16 + 10 + 16$$

$$= 42$$

Area and Perimeter of T-shape

The T-shape consists of two rectangles joined together to form a T-like structure.

Area of the T-shape:

To find the total area of the T-shape, we need to calculate the areas of both rectangles and then add them together.

$$\text{Area of Rectangle 1} = \text{Length} \times \text{Width}$$

$$\text{Area of Rectangle 2} = \text{Length} \times \text{Width}$$

$$\text{Total Area} = \text{Area of Rectangle 1} + \text{Area of Rectangle 2}$$

The perimeter of the T-shape is the sum of the perimeters of the two rectangles, minus the length of the overlapping side:

$$Perimeter = 2(l1+w1) + 2(l2+w2) - (w1-w2)$$

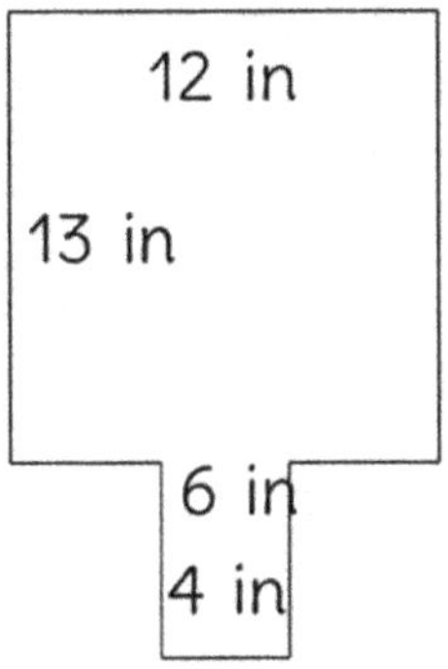

Area= 12 × 13 + 6 × 4

Area= 156 + 24

Area= 180 in^2

Perimeter= 2(12+13) +2(6+4) − (12-4)

Perimeter=2(25) + 2(10) − 8

Perimeter= 50 + 20 − 8

Perimeter= 62 in^2

<u>**Area and Perimeter of Parallelogram**</u>

A parallelogram is a four-sided polygon with opposite sides that are parallel and equal in length. To find the area and perimeter of a parallelogram, we use specific formulas based on its dimensions.

For example:

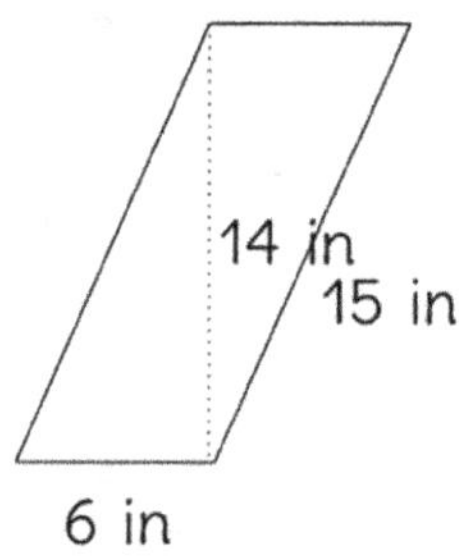

Let's denote:

- The length of one side of the parallelogram as $a = 15$.

- The length of an adjacent side (parallel to a) $b = 6$.

- The height of the parallelogram (perpendicular distance between the two parallel sides) as $h=14$

Area of Parallelogram

$$\text{Area= Base} \times \text{Height}$$

$$\text{Area=}6 \times 1\ 4$$

$$\text{Area=}84$$

Perimeter of Parallelogram

$$2(a + b)$$

$$= 2(15+6)$$

$$= 2(21)$$

$$= 42$$

<u>Area and Perimeter of Trapezoids</u>

A trapezoid is a quadrilateral with at least one pair of parallel sides. To find the area and perimeter of a trapezoid, we use specific formulas based on its dimensions.

For example:

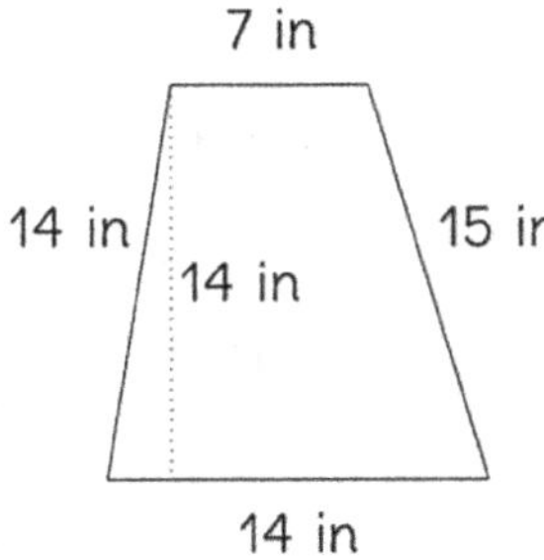

Let's denote:

- The lengths of the parallel sides of the trapezoid as $a = 7$ and $b = 14$.

- The lengths of the non-parallel sides as $c = 14$ and $d = 15$.

- The height of the trapezoid (the perpendicular distance between the parallel sides) as $h=14$.

Area of the Trapezoid:

The area of a trapezoid is given by the formula:

$$\text{Area} = \frac{1}{2} \times \text{Height} \times (\text{Sum of the lengths of the parallel sides})$$

$$\text{Area} = \frac{1}{2} \times h \times (a + b)$$

$$\text{Area} = \frac{1}{2} \times 14 \times (7 + 14)$$

$$\text{Area} = \frac{1}{2} \times 14 \times 21$$

$$\text{Area} = 147 \text{ in}^2$$

Perimeter of the Trapezoid:

$$\text{Perimeter} = 7 + 14 + 14 + 15$$

$$= 50 \text{ in}^2$$

Pythagorean Theorem

The Pythagorean Theorem is a fundamental principle in geometry that relates the lengths of the sides of a right triangle. It states that in any right triangle, the square of the length of the hypotenuse (the side opposite the right angle) is equal to the sum of the squares of the lengths of the other two sides.

$$a2 + b2 = c2$$

Let's use the Pythagorean Theorem to find the length of the hypotenuse (c) when $a=44$ and $b=78$.

$$c^2 = 44^2 + 78^2$$
$$c^2 = 1936 + 6084 \qquad c = \sqrt{8020}$$
$$c^2 = 8020 \qquad c \approx 89.554$$

Volume and surface Area

Volume refers to the amount of space occupied by a three-dimensional object. For shapes like cubes or rectangular prisms, we calculate volume by multiplying their length, width, and height.

To find the volume V of a rectangular prism, we use the formula:

$$Volume = length \; x \; width \; x \; height$$

Surface Area represents the total area covering all the faces of a three-dimensional object. For shapes like cubes or rectangular prisms, we find the surface area by summing the areas of all its faces.

The formula for surface area *SA* of a cube or rectangular prism is:

$$Surface\ Area\ =\ 2lw\ +\ 2lh\ +\ 2wh$$

Where: *l* is the length, *w* is the width, and *h* is the height of the object.

For example: Let's find the Volume and Surface Area of following rectangular prisms:

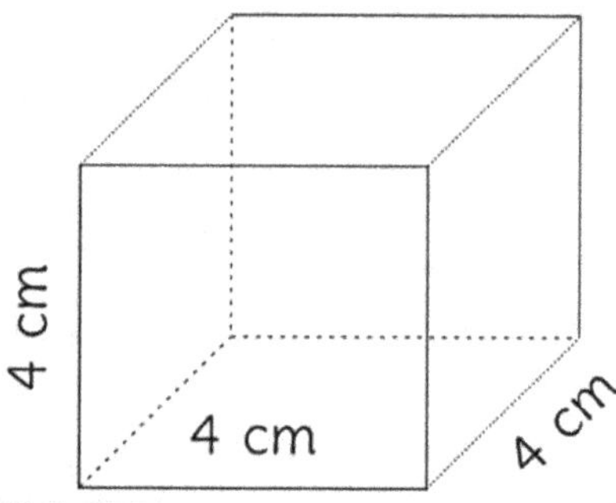

$$Volume\ =\ length\ \times\ width\ \times\ height$$

$$=\ 4 \times 4 \times 4$$

$$=\ 64\ cm^2$$

$$Surface\ Area\ =\ 2lw\ +\ 2lh\ +\ 2wh$$

$$=\ 2(4 \times 4) + 2(4 \times 4) + 2(4 \times 4)$$

$$=\ 32 + 32 + 32$$

$$=\ 96\ cm2$$

Different 3D objects have unique formulas for finding their volume and surface area. Here are some common ones:

1. Cube:

- Volume: $V = s^3$ (where s is the length of one side of the cube)

- Surface area: $SA = 6s^2$

2. Sphere:

- Volume: $V = (\frac{4}{3})\pi r^3$ (where r is the radius of the sphere)

- Surface area: $SA = 4\pi r^2$

3. Cone:

- Volume: $V = (\frac{1}{3})\pi r^2 h$ (where r is the radius of the base and h is the height of the cone)

- Surface area: $SA = \pi r^2 + \pi r\sqrt{(r^2 + h^2)}$

4. Cylinder:

- Volume: $V = \pi r^2 h$ (where r is the radius of the base and h is the height of the cylinder)

- Surface area: $SA = 2\pi r^2 + 2\pi rh$

5. Pyramid:

- Volume: $V = (\frac{1}{3})Bh$ (where B is the area of the base and h is the height of the pyramid)

- Surface area: $SA = B + \frac{1}{2}Pl$ (where P is the perimeter of the base and l is the slant height of the pyramid)

Equations (Two Sides)

Solve for the variable.

① $2y = 9 - y$

② $5 + 4z = 45 - z$

③ $5k + 10 = 9k + 2$

④ $14 - 3x = 6x + 5$

⑤ $8k = 63 + k$

⑥ $6 + z = 4z$

⑦ $30 + k = 4 + 4k + 5$

⑧ $5z + 7 = 63 - 3z$

⑨ $1 + 3y + 7 = 36 - y$

10 $36 - k = 4 + 7k$

11 $7 - x = 2x + 1$

12 $42 - x = 6x$

13 $4 + 8y + 9 = 58 - y$

14 $4 + 4x + 9 = 38 - x$

⑮ $5y + 2 = 2y + 20$

⑯ $2k + 3 = 15 - k$

⑰ $12 - m = 5m$

① $4 + 6y + 4 = 22 - y + 7$

⑲ $21 + m + 1 = 3 + 3m + 7$

20 $17 + y = 6 + 2y + 5$

21 $8x + 5 = 68 - x$

22 $46 + y = 2 + 7y + 2$

23 $18 - x + 7 = 9 + 3x + 4$

24 $43 - z + 14 = 6 + 5z + 3$

25) $3 + 3x + 8 = 29 - x + 10$

26) $7x + 7 = 19 - 5x$

27) $8 + 7y + 8 = 22 + y$

28) $1 + y = 2y$

29) $28 - m = 4 + 2m$

Simplify Expressions

① $4 + 3m + 3 + 2m$

② $3y - 2y + 8 + 1$

③ $7k + 2 + 3k + 2 + 2k + 5$

④ $2 - 5(y - 7)$

⑤ $-7k + 6 - 7k$

⑥ $-9y - 1 + 6y$

⑦ $-7z - 2z$

⑧ $-7k - 6 + 9k$

⑨ $3z + 8 + 3z$

10 $7 + 9(4z - 8)$

1 $2 - 3(2m - 9)$

12 $-4 - 4x + 4x - 7 + 6x$

13 $4x - 4x + 4 + 3$

14 $y + 4y$

(15) $3m + 5 + 4m + 5 + 2m + 2$

(16) $8 + 6 + 7y - 8y + 3 - 9y$

(17) $8m - 6m + m - 5 + 6$

(1) $-3y + 2 - 4 + 3y$

(19) $1 + x - 6 + 9x$

20) $x - x + 7x + 6 + 1$

21) $-4z - 7 - 9z$

22) $-7y + 8y + 6 - 7y$

23) $-2k + 8 + 4k$

24) $5k + 9 - 8 - 2k + 6k$

25) $7 + k + 6 + 2k$

26) $-2 - 4k + 5k - 8 + 2k$

27) $7 + 8k - 2 + 5k - 8 + 8k$

28) $7z + z$

29) $x + 7 - 4 - 9x + 6x$

Order of Operations (PEMDAS)

Evaluate Expressions.

① $10 \times 2 \times 7 =$

② $8 + 8 + 3 =$

③ $(5^2) \times (8^2) + 7 =$

④ $10 + 3 + 10 =$

⑤ $4 + 6 + 9 =$

⑥ $5(4 + 2) =$

⑦ $5 + 7 + 6 =$

⑧ $9 + 10^2 + 7 + 1^2 =$

⑨ $9 \times 6 =$

⑩ $10 \times 9 =$

① $(10^2) \times (9^2) + 8 =$

⑫ $6 \times 4 + 5 =$

⑬ $1 \times 6 + 2 =$

⑭ $5 + 9 + 7 + 8 =$

⑮ $7 + 8 + 9 =$

⑯ $4 \times 10 =$

⑰ $(10 + 1) \times (4 + 6) =$

① $1 + 3 - 4 + 1 =$

19 $1 + 3^2 + 1 + 8^2 =$

20 $(9 \times 8) - (5 + 10) =$

21 $(7 + 2)(5 + 5) =$

22 $(10 + 1)(9 + 9) =$

23 $3 \times 8 =$

24 $(7^2) \times (10^2) + 9 =$

25 $(2 \times 3) - (8 + 7) =$

26 $10 \times 7 =$

27 $9(5 + 4) =$

28 $8 \times (6 + 2) =$

Simplifying Equations

Simplify the following equations when the value of $z = 4$

① $z - (-10) =$

② $z - 1 =$

③ $-1 - z =$

④ $9 + z =$

⑤ $z - 10 =$

⑥ $7 + z =$

⑦ $z + (-5) =$

⑧ $z + 0 =$

Simplifying Equations

Simplify the following equations when the value of z = -10

① $z - 10 =$

② $z - (-9) =$

③ $2 + z =$

④ $z - (-1) =$

⑤ $z + (-6) =$

⑥ $-1 - z =$

⑦ $9 - z =$

⑧ $z - (-4) =$

Simplifying Equations

Simplify the following equations when the value of $z = -9$

① $-7 + z =$

② $5 + z =$

③ $-5 - z =$

④ $z - 5 =$

⑤ $10 - z =$

⑥ $z + 6 =$

⑦ $z - 3 =$

⑧ $-10 - z =$

Simplifying Equations

Simplify the following equations when the value of $k = -9$

① $k - 1 =$

② $-4 - k =$

③ $6 - k =$

④ $k + (-8) =$

⑤ $k - 3 =$

⑥ $-8 - k =$

⑦ $k + (-5) =$

⑧ $k - (-7) =$

Solving Inequalities

① $7 > 7 + m$

② $\dfrac{z}{-5} \leq -2$

③ $4 < 1 - y$

④ $-18 \geq 15\,m$

⑤

$$-5 > \dfrac{y}{2}$$

⑥

$$-7y < 3$$

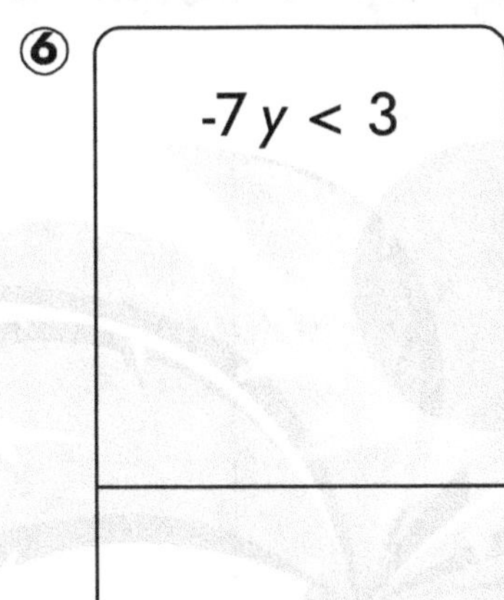

⑦

$$z + -1 > -10$$

⑧

$$6 \leq k - -1$$

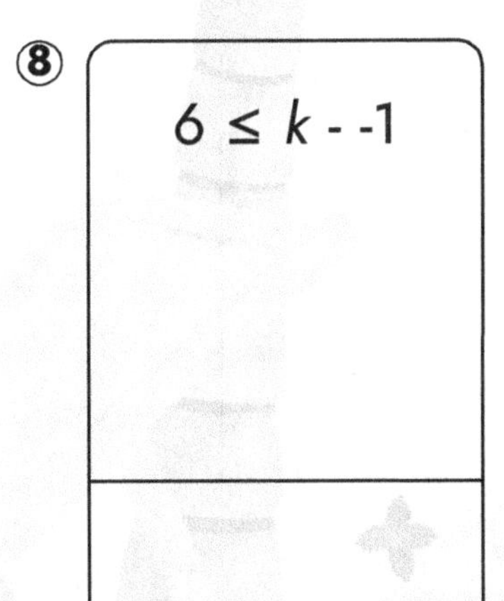

⑨

$$8 - x \geq 9$$

⑩

$$2 < \frac{k}{6}$$

①

$$-8\,y \geq -10$$

⑫

$$y + -3 \leq -7$$

13 $-5 - z < 7$

14 $-4 \geq 2 + z$

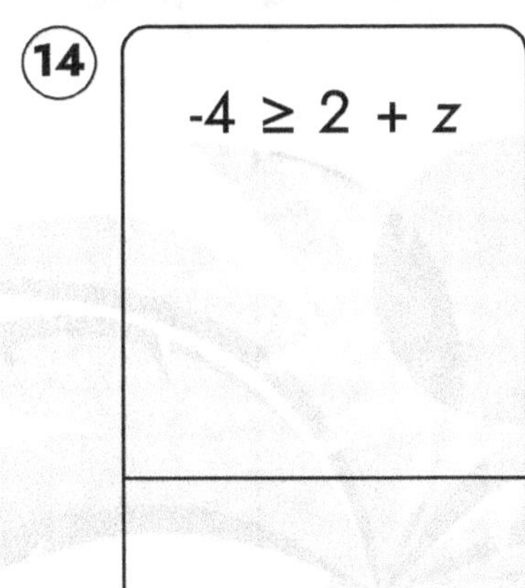

15 $-16 < -4\,m$

16 $-6 \leq \dfrac{k}{-5}$

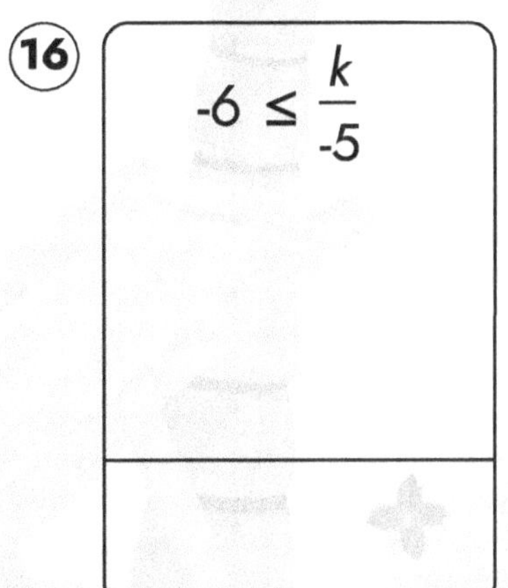

⑰ $y + \text{-}10 \leq 7$

① $\text{-}5\,k < 6$

⑲ $\text{-}2 > \dfrac{m}{\text{-}5}$

⑳ $9 < k - 7$

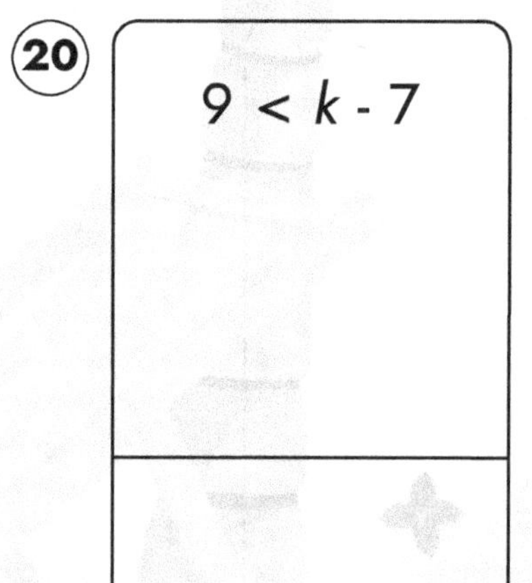

21

$$y - \text{-}7 < \text{-}1$$

22

$$9x \leq \text{-}9$$

23

$$\frac{m}{2} \geq 6$$

24

$$y + \text{-}5 > \text{-}7$$

Standard Linear Equations

1. $-4x + 4 = -32$

5. $-6x + 7 = 55$

2. $-1x + -2 = -12$

6. $8x + -6 = -38$

3. $10x + 2 = 12$

7. $8x + -4 = 4$

4. $-3x + -6 = 3$

8. $6x + 4 = 22$

9. -3x + -1 = 26

13. 5x + 8 = 13

10. -6x + 8 = -40

14. 9x + 9 = -36

11. -1x + -2 = 4

15. -9x + -4 = -22

12. -9x + 4 = -59

16. -7x + 4 = 18

17. -6x + 10 = 70

18. -4x + -10 = 2

19. 5x + -1 = 49

20. -4x + 10 = -2

System of Equations

11. $7x + 9y = 1$

$1x + 6y = 2$

2. $5x + 5y = 5$

$6x + 10y = 1$

3. $9x + 5y = 1$

$2x + 2y = 6$

4. $1x + 10y = 8$

$3x + 6y = 6$

5. $10x + 4y = 6$

$5x + 8y = 8$

6. $5x + 10y = 3$

$10x + 7y = 4$

7. $8x + 2y = 3$

$6x + 8y = 2$

8. $6x + 1y = 1$

$4x + 1y = 7$

9. $2x + 3y = 2$

$3x + 5y = 5$

10. $4x + 8y = 10$

$6x + 7y = 9$

11. $10x + 5y = 6$

$7x + 1y = 4$

12. $6x + 6y = 3$

$8x + 4y = 3$

Verbal Algebra Expressions

① Six times a number equals 4 less than eight times the number. What is the number?

② One less than eight times a number is 23. Find the number.

③ Find two consecutive even integers such that four times the smaller decreased by the larger is 10.

④ Twenty-six more than the second of three consecutive even integers is the same as the difference between the third and ten times the first. Find the numbers.

⑤ The sum of the largest and five times the smallest of three consecutive numbers is equal to 32. Find the numbers.

⑥ If the product of ten and a number is increased by 5, the result is 105. Find the number?

⑦ One number is five times another. Their sum is 30. Find the numbers.

⑧ One number is two times another. Their sum is 27. Find the numbers.

9 The sum of the first and third of three consecutive numbers is 14. Find the numbers.

10 The difference of two numbers is 45. The larger number is 9 more than five times the smaller number. What are the numbers?

1 One less than twice a number is 15. Find the number.

12 Two-fourths of a number diminished by 1 is 1. Find the number.

13   When a number is divided by five, the result is 5. What is the number?

14   One less than five times a number is 24. Find the number.

15   The product of two numbers is 40. One number is three less than the other. What are the numbers?

16   Two-thirds of a number is 4. Find the number.

17   A number increased by one is 7. Find the number.

1   The sum of two numbers is 17. One number is nine less than the other. Find the numbers.

19   The sum of four consecutive numbers is 34. What are the numbers?

20   A number decreased by 9 is 3. Find the number.

21   The sum of two consecutive numbers is 7. What are the numbers?

22 The greater of two numbers is 2 less than five times the smaller number. Their sum is 16. Find the numbers.

23 The sum of two numbers is 24. The larger number is seven times the smaller number. What are the numbers?

24 One of two numbers is two-fourths of the other number. The sum of the numbers is 6. Find the numbers.

25 The difference of a number and one is equal to 7. What is the number?

Percent

Calculate the given percent of each value.

① ⬚ of 924 = 33.264

② 0.6% of 66 = ⬚

③ ⬚ of 3 = 0.015

④ ⬚ of 4 = 0.032

⑤ 0.3% of ⬚ = 0.006

⑥ ⬚ of 57 = 10.146

⑦ 7.5% of ⬚ = 0.225

⑧ ⬚ of 131 = 0.524

9   9.0% of 924 = ☐

10   0.8% of ☐ = 0.152

1   ☐ of 5 = 1.74

12   ☐ of 392 = 1.96

13   ☐ of 4 = 0.124

14   0.3% of ☐ = 1.221

15   0.6% of 8 = ☐

16   37.4% of 51 = ☐

17   7.7% of 6 = ☐

1   ☐ of 356 = 1.424

19 ⬚ of 2 = 0.012

20 0.4% of 78 = ⬚

21 2.0% of 893 = ⬚

22 4.0% of 43 = ⬚

23 ⬚ of 709 = 1.418

24 19.0% of ⬚ = 14.63

25 ⬚ of 64 = 5.888

26 0.5% of 21 = ⬚

27 ⬚ of 2 = 0.138

28 0.3% of 343 = ⬚

Convert: Ratio, Fraction, Percent, and Decimals

①

	Ratio	Fraction	Percent	Decimal
a.	2:20			
b.			26.7%	
c.		1/1		
d.	6:7			
e.				0.429
f.		7/13		
g.			16.7%	
h.				0.214
i.		2/5		
j.	2:9			
k.				0.895
l.		2/8		
m.		5/12		
n.				0.643
o.	2:3			

②

	Ratio	Fraction	Percent	Decimal
a.	6:7			
b.				0.133
c.		1/2		
d.				0.062
e.				0.071
f.	19:20			
g.		1/3		
h.		3/11		
i.				0.867
j.	9:10			
k.			100%	
l.	16:18			
m.		2/8		
n.				0.833
o.				0.429

③

	Ratio	Fraction	Percent	Decimal
a.			100%	
b.			50%	
c.	5:7			
d.				0.5
e.				0.444
f.			50%	
g.		9/18		
h.		6/17		
i.				0.333
j.			57.1%	
k.	14:15			
l.				0.2
m.		11/18		
n.	2:14			
o.				0.167

④

	Ratio	Fraction	Percent	Decimal
a.	8:15			
b.			100%	
c.			25%	
d.		9/20		
e.		1/17		
f.		6/7		
g.		7/18		
h.		9/13		
i.				0.438
j.				0.538
k.				0.364
l.				0.938
m.			87.5%	
n.	9:12			
o.			91.7%	

⑤

	Ratio	Fraction	Percent	Decimal
a.	8:17			
b.				0.667
c.	15:19			
d.			100%	
e.		7/11		
f.			36.4%	
g.	4:7			
h.			81.2%	
i.			50%	
j.	9:14			
k.			92.3%	
l.	8:14			
m.			33.3%	
n.				0.188
o.				0.4

Plotting Lines

Plot and draw the lines.

① 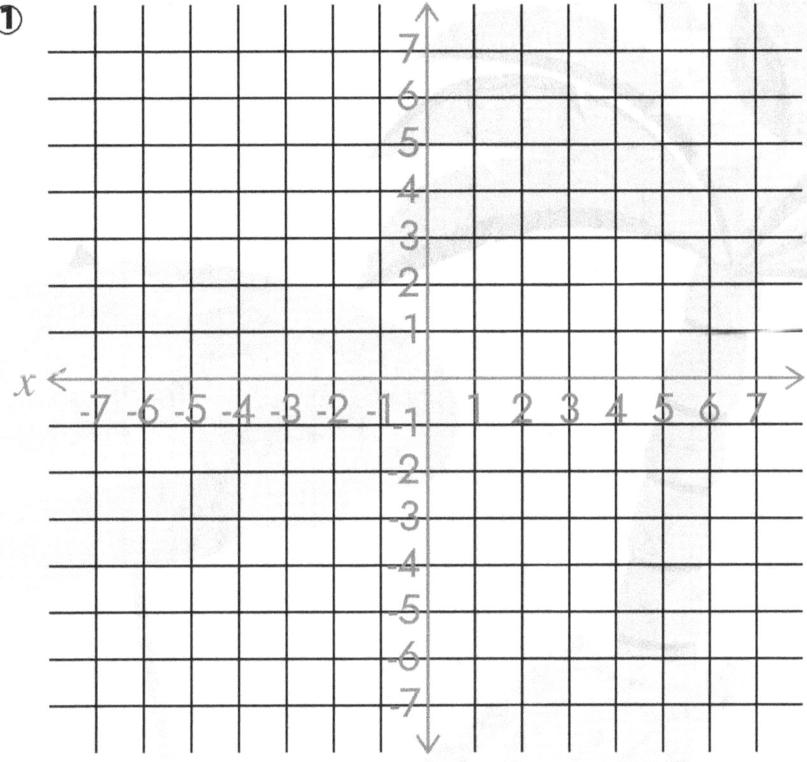

A = (-1, -7) B = (5, -1)

C = (7, 1) D = (0, -6)

E = (6, 0) F = (3, -3)

②

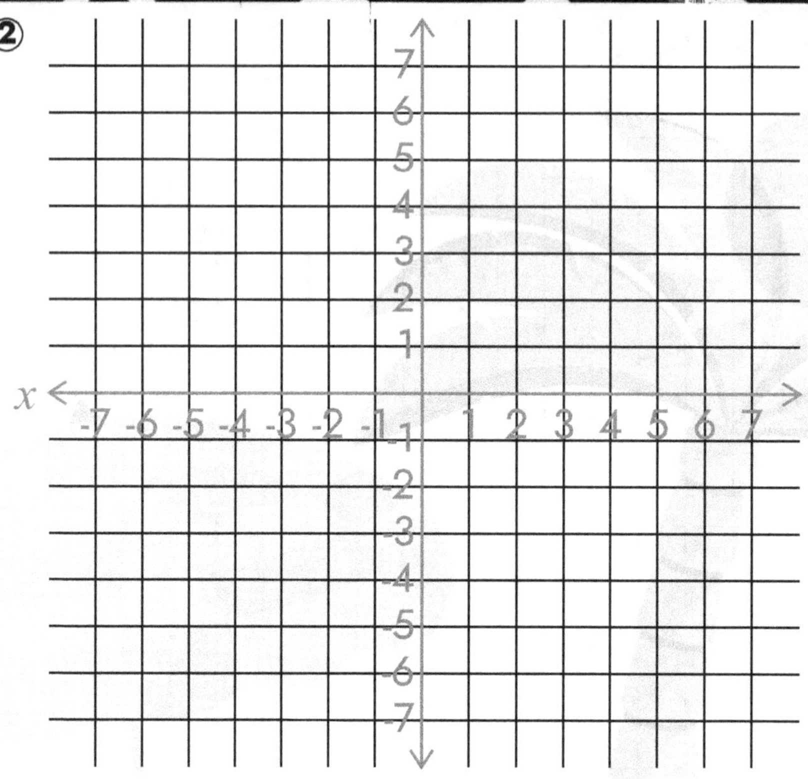

A = (0, -4)   B = (7, -4)

C = (-3, -4)   D = (-2, -4)

E = (5, -4)   F = (6, -4)

③ 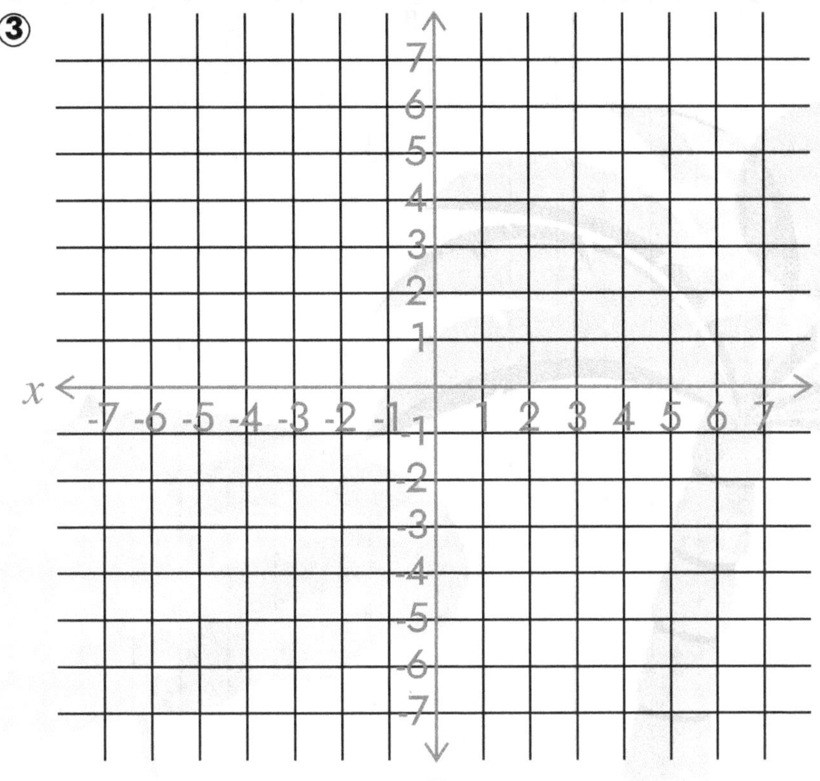

A = (2, -5)   B = (6, -1)

C = (0, -7)   D = (7, 0)

E = (1, -6)   F = (3, -4)

④

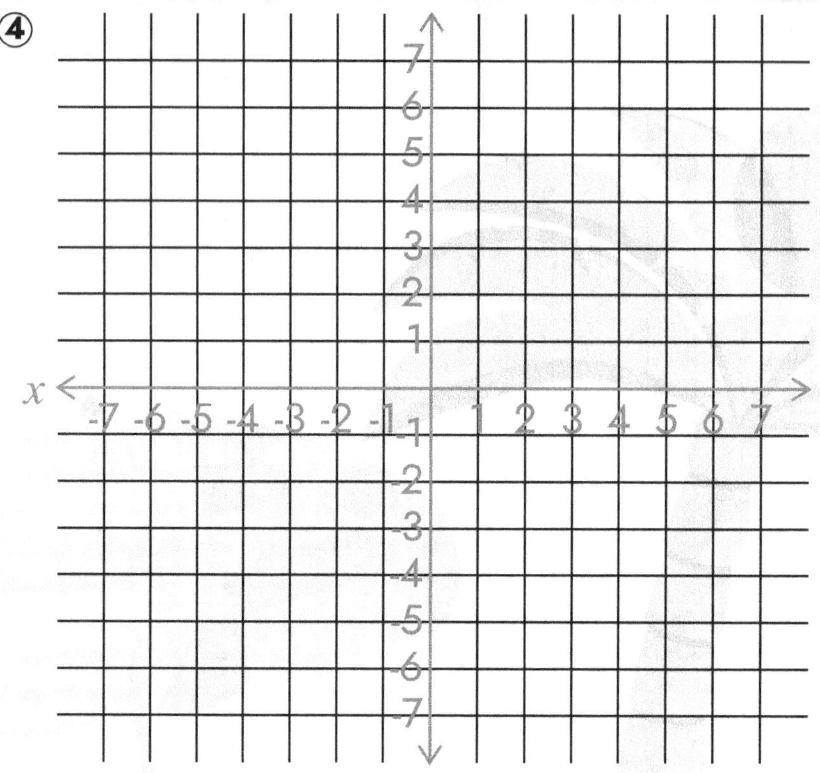

A = (1, 0)   B = (3, -4)

C = (2, -2)   D = (-2, 6)

E = (-1, 4)   F = (0, 2)

⑤

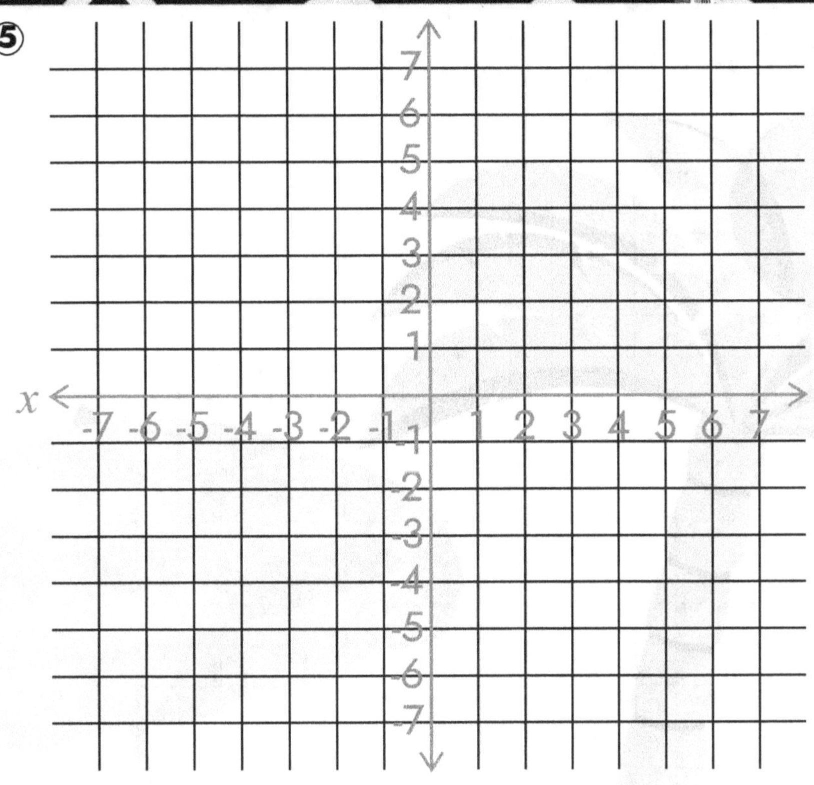

A = (2, -6)   B = (0, -5)

C = (-4, -3)   D = (4, -7)

E = (-6, -2)   F = (-2, -4)

Graphing Linear Equations

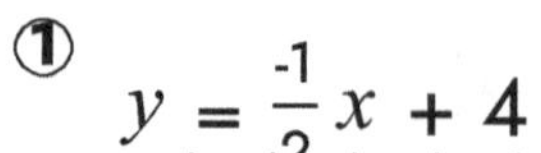

① $y = \dfrac{-1}{2}x + 4$

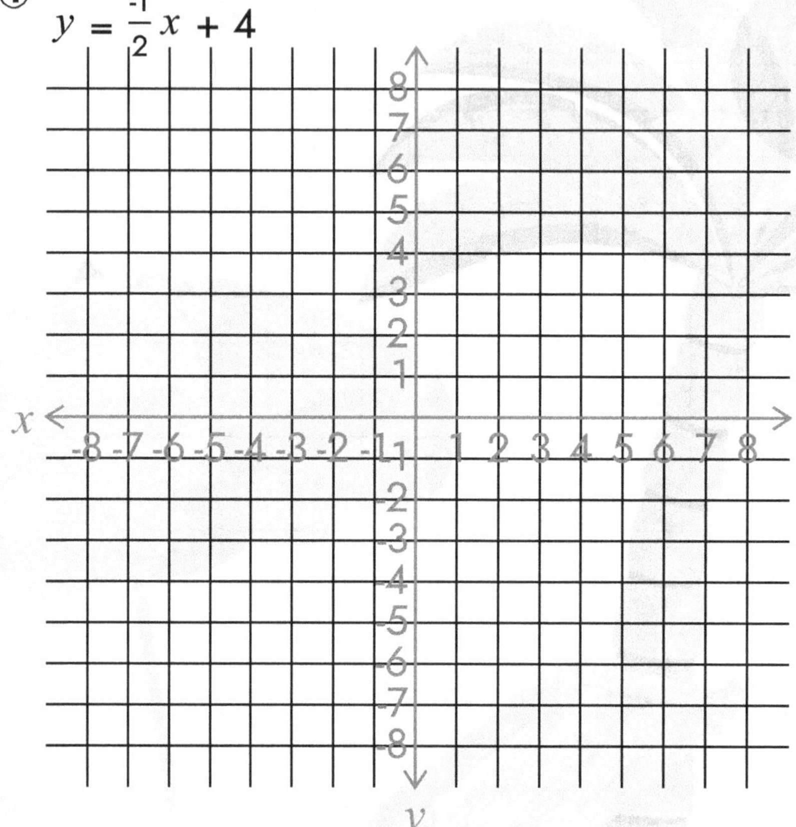

② $y = \dfrac{^-9}{4}x + 2$

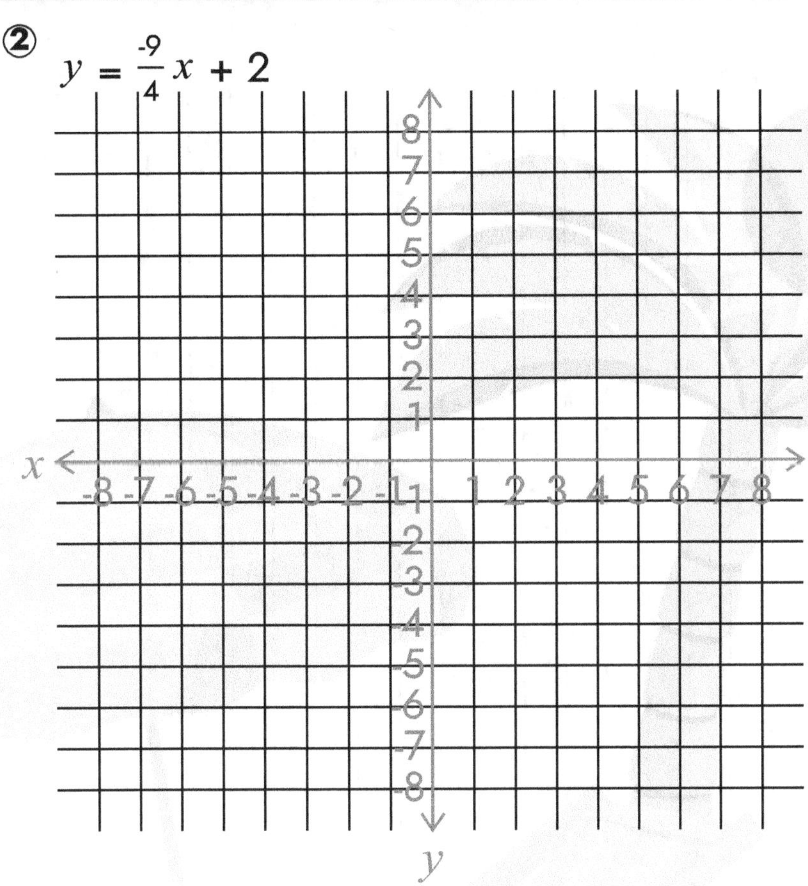

③ $y = \dfrac{5}{4}x + 6$

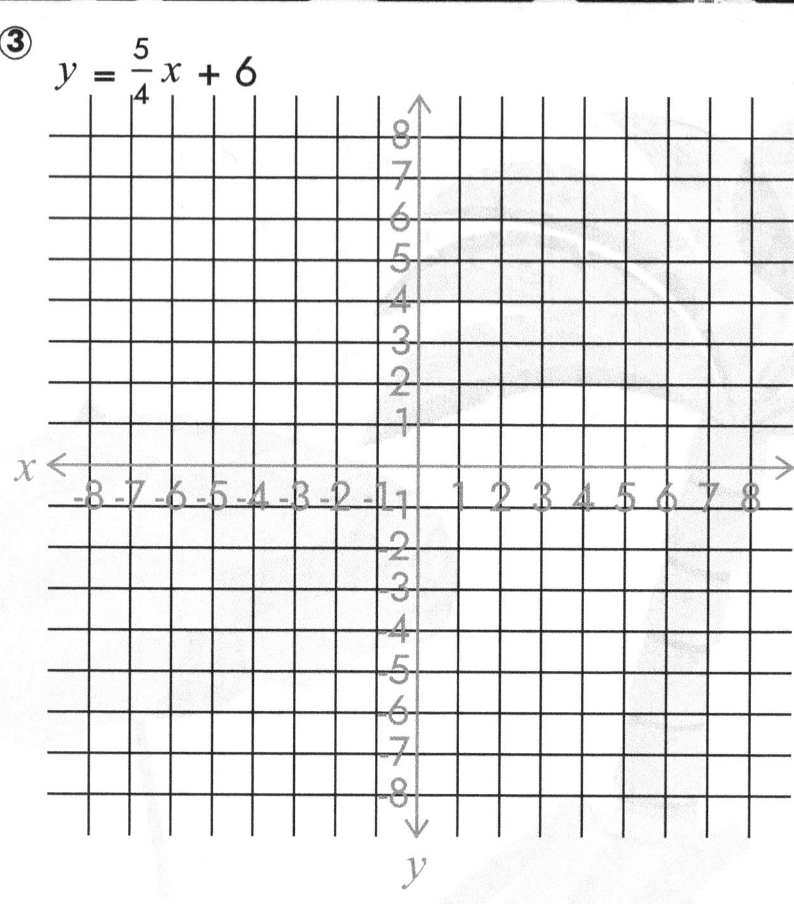

④ $y = \dfrac{7}{4}x - 2$

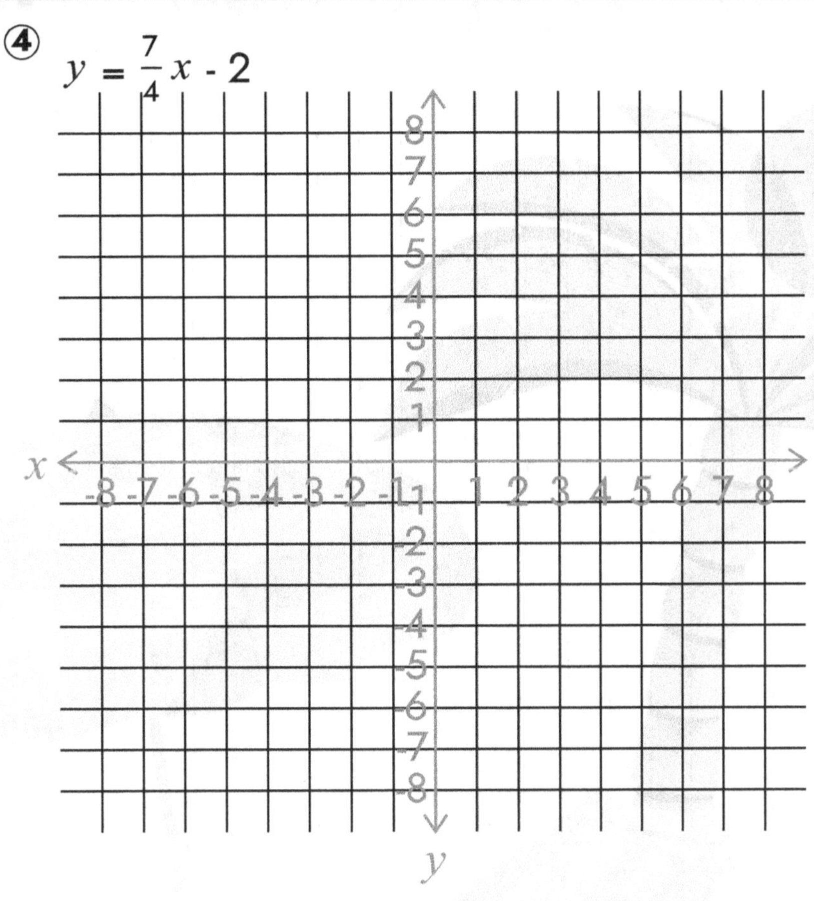

⑤ $y = \dfrac{-7}{4} x - 5$

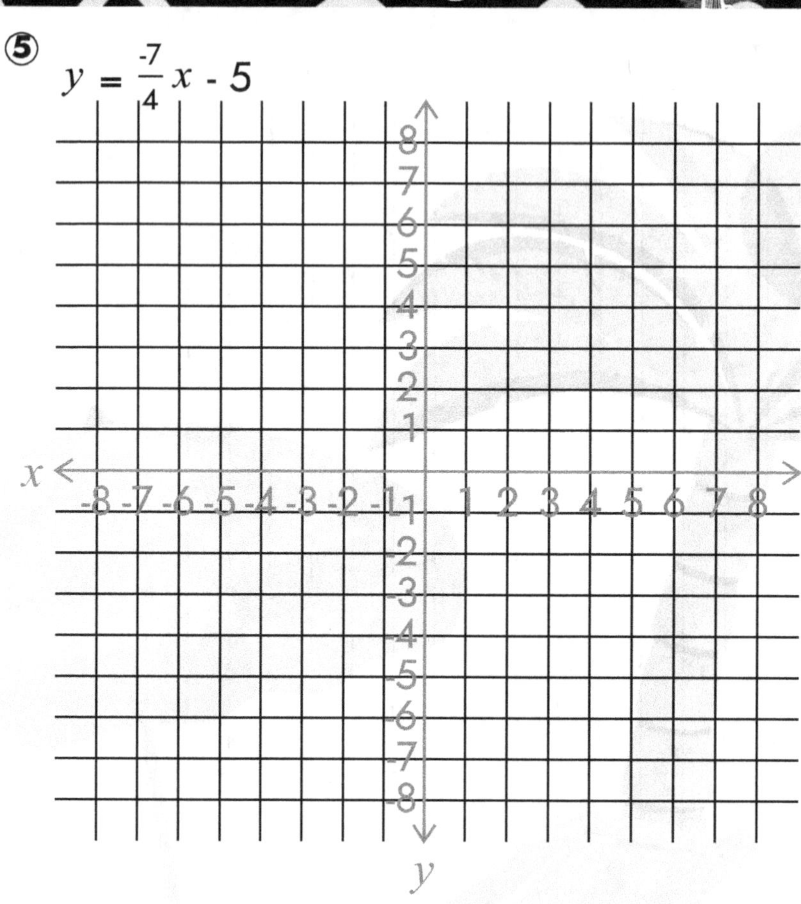

Cartesian Coordinates

Plot the points.

① 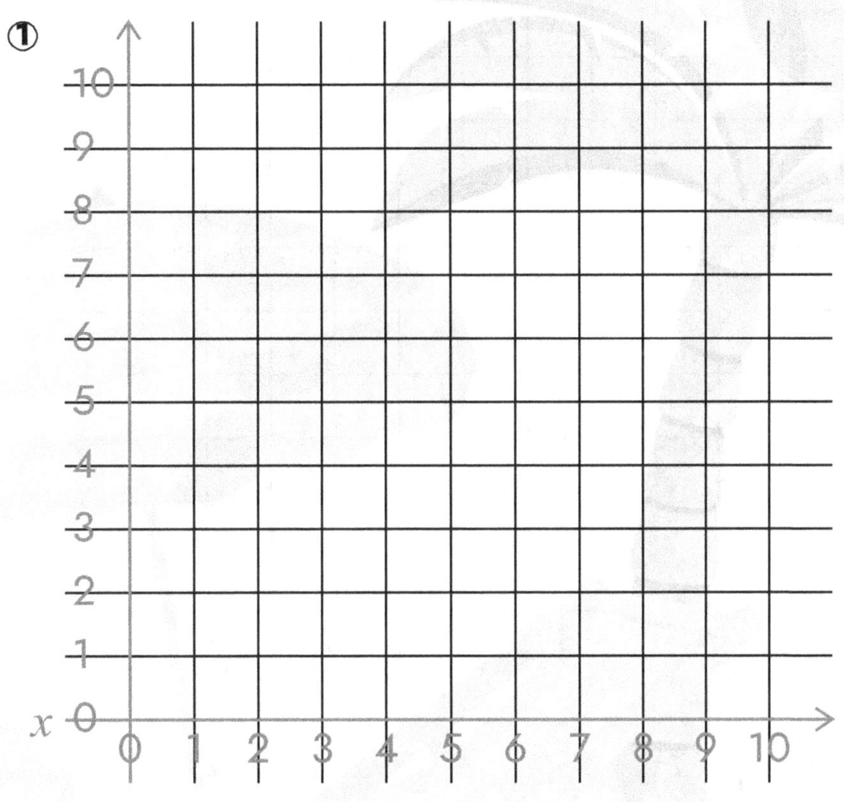

A = (5, 0)   B = (7, 0)   C = (3, 2)

D = (6, 9)   E = (4, 4)   F = (9, 10)

G = (10, 8)   H = (9, 4)   I = (0, 10)

② 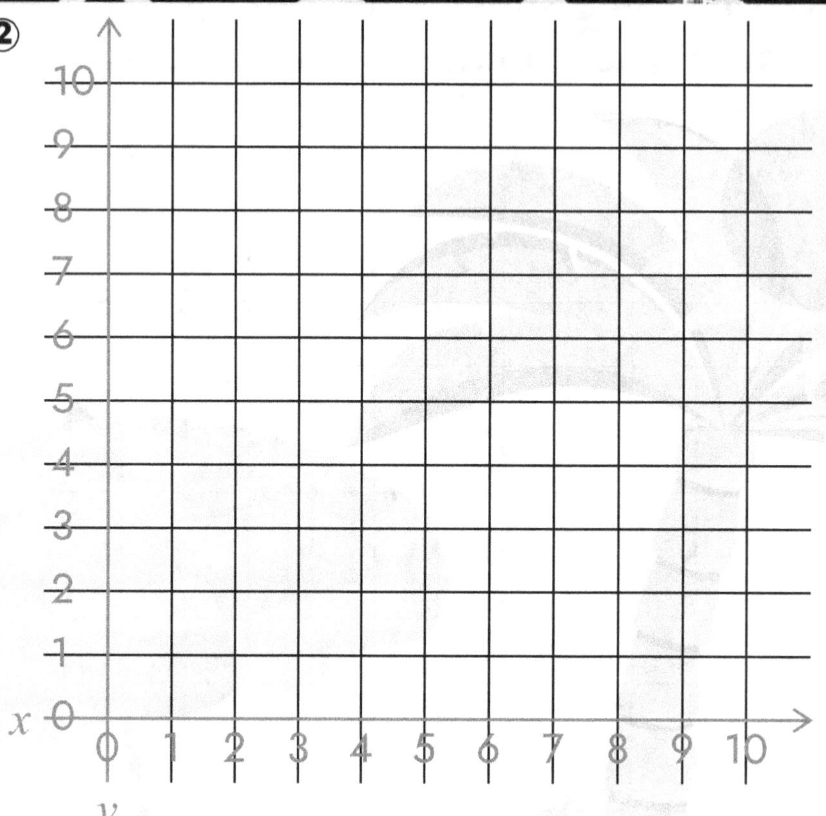

A = (5, 2)   B = (8, 8)   C = (5, 0)

D = (8, 5)   E = (7, 6)   F = (5, 7)

G = (10, 5)   H = (6, 10)   I = (10, 10)

③

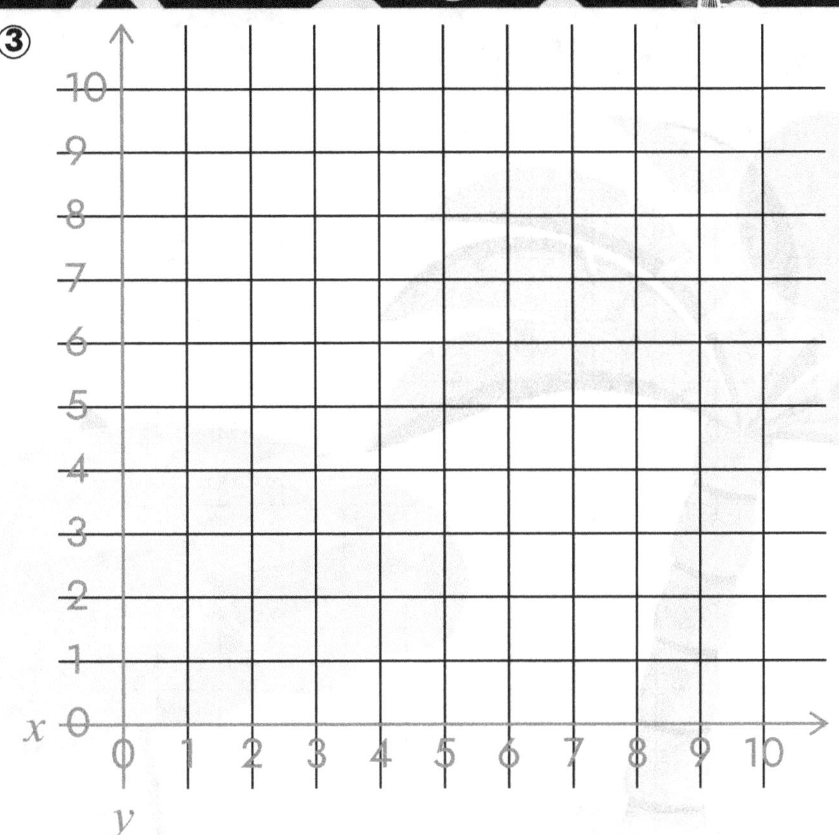

A = (7, 10)   B = (0, 8)   C = (6, 0)

D = (3, 5)   E = (8, 4)   F = (8, 2)

G = (2, 9)   H = (3, 2)   I = (3, 10)

Cartesian Coordinates

Plot the points.

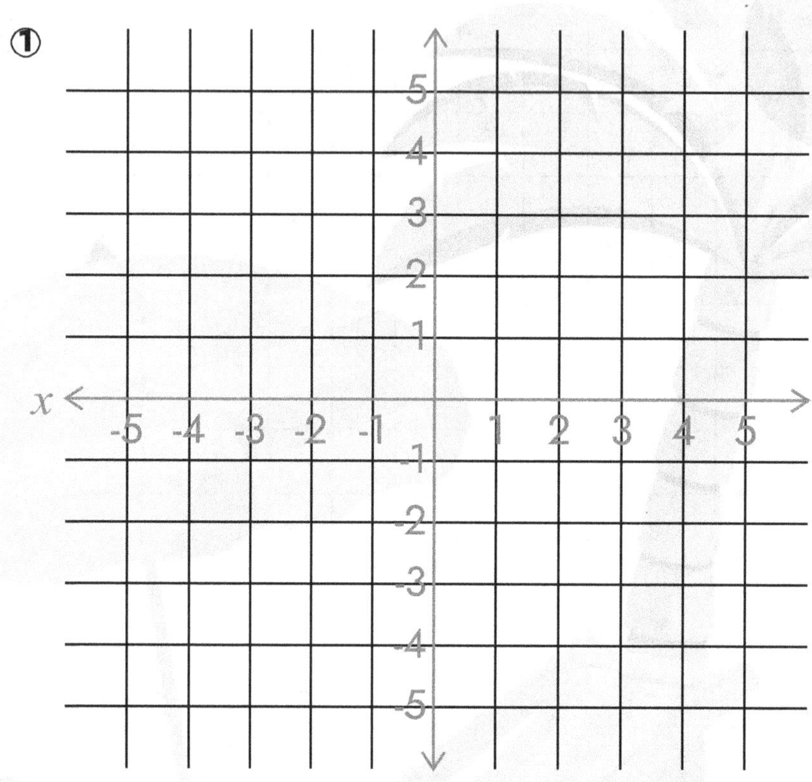

A = (0, -2)   B = (0, -4)   C = (-4, 3)

D = (5, -3)   E = (5, 0)   F = (-4, 4)

G = (0, 2)   H = (-3, -5)   I = (5, 3)

②

A = (2, 2)   B = (-1, -5)   C = (-3, -1)

D = (2, -1)   E = (-2, 1)   F = (-2, 2)

G = (3, -1)   H = (2, -5)   I = (-1, -1)

③

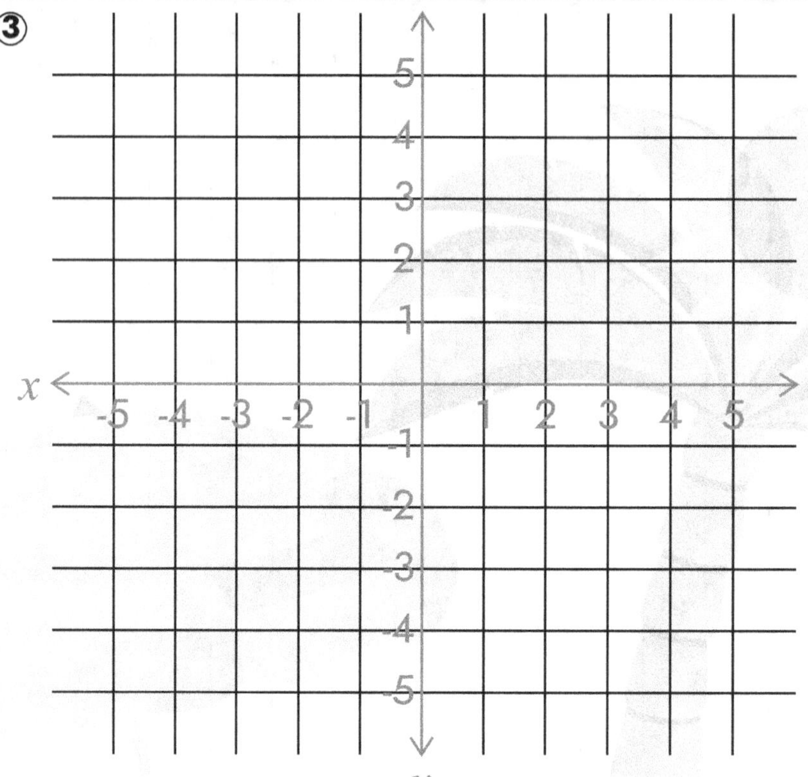

A = (0, 4)   B = (1, 3)   C = (-4, -4)

D = (0, -2)   E = (-3, 5)   F = (3, 1)

G = (2, -3)   H = (-2, 5)   I = (0, 2)

Area and Perimeter

① 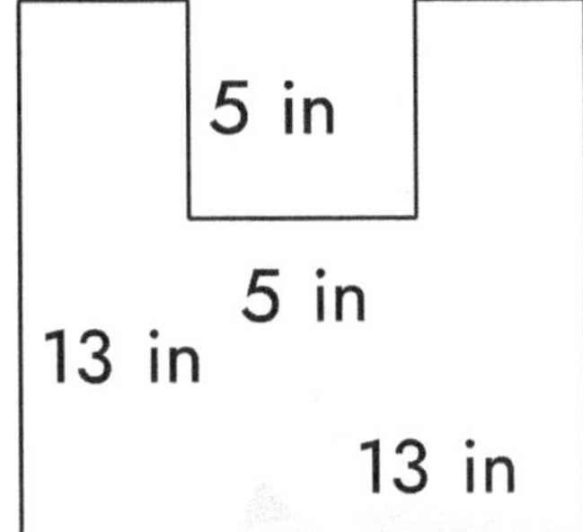

② 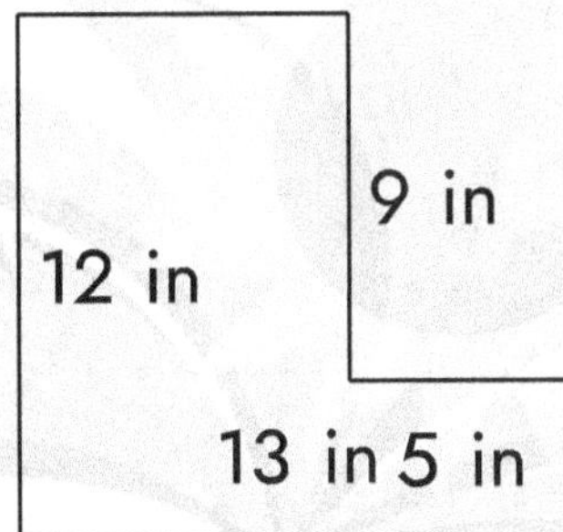

③ 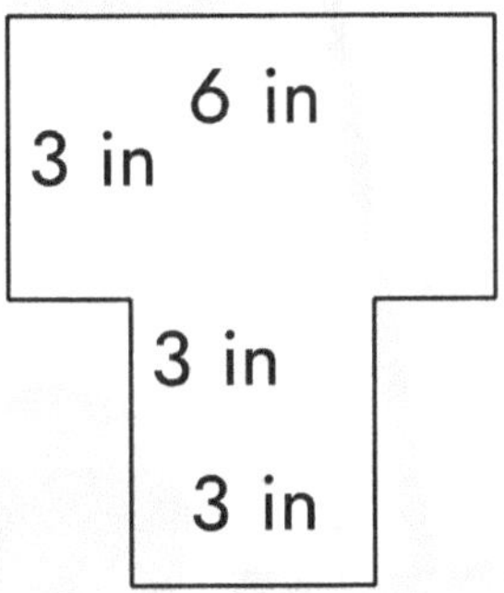

④ 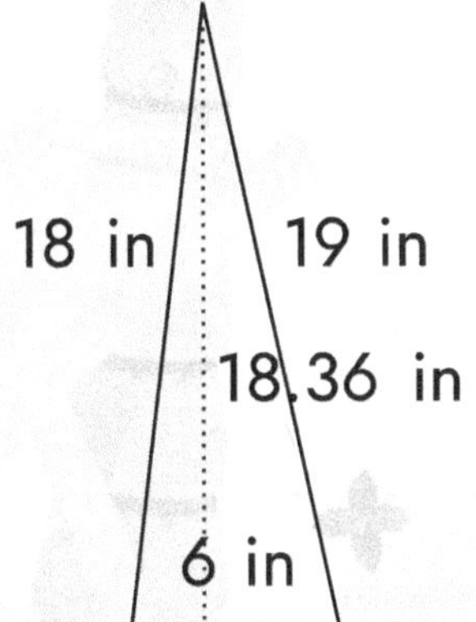

⑤

7 in

7 in

3 in

⑥ 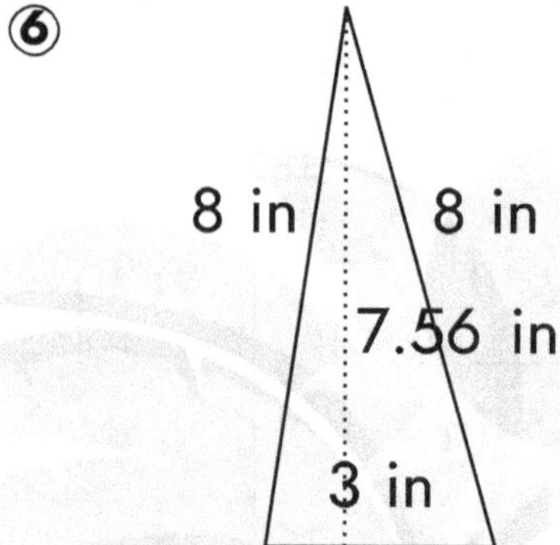

8 in   8 in

7.56 in

3 in

⑦ 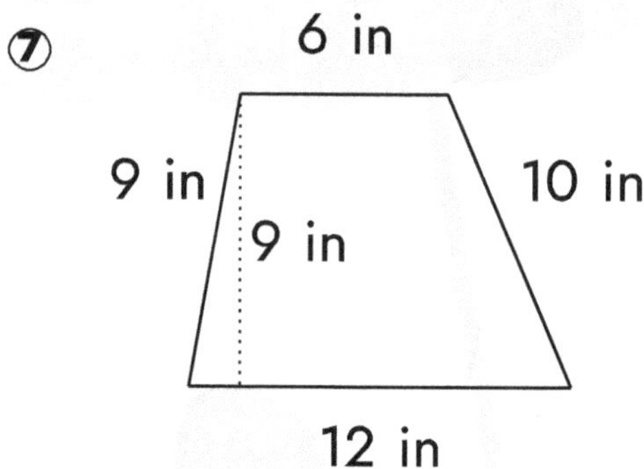

6 in

9 in   10 in

9 in

12 in

⑧ 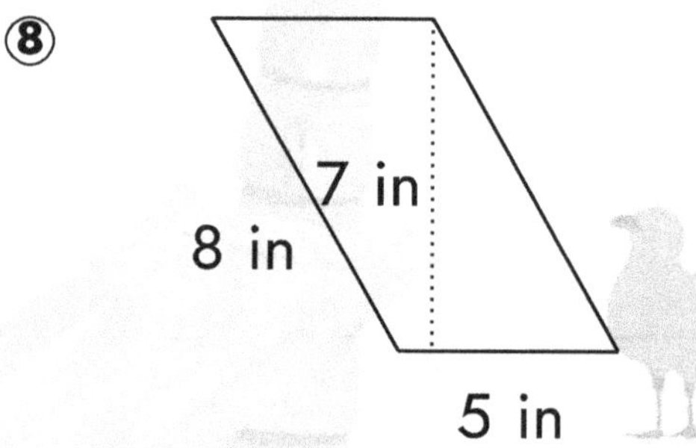

7 in

8 in

5 in

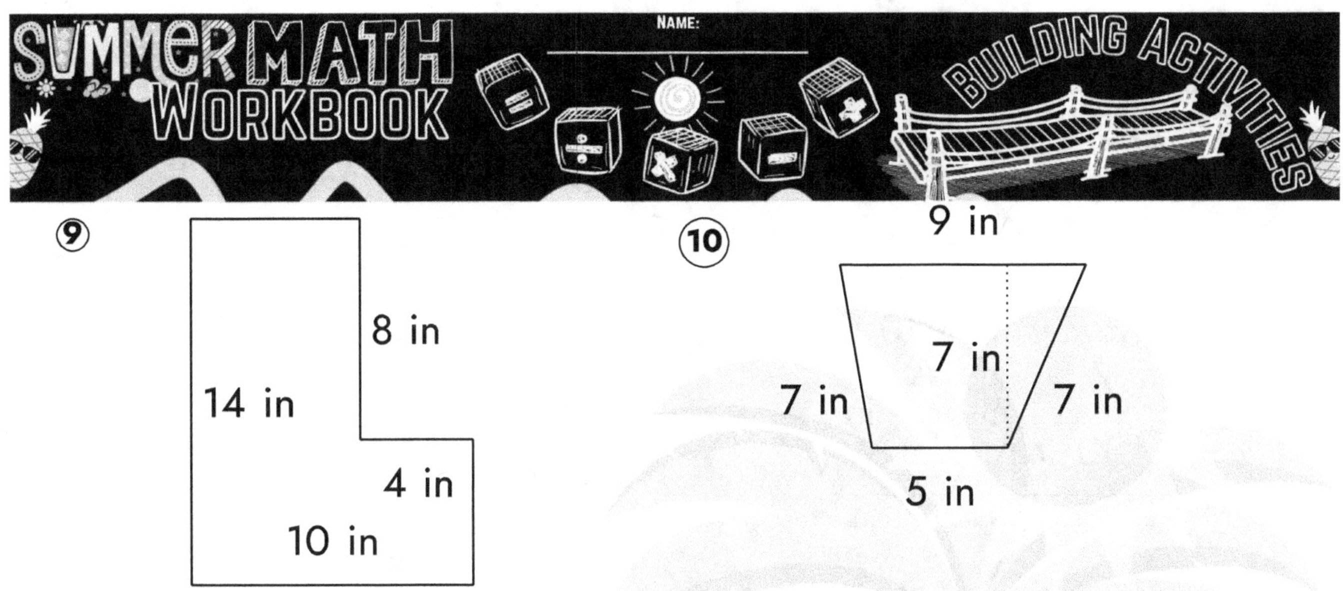

⑨

8 in
14 in
4 in
10 in

⑩

9 in
7 in
7 in
7 in
5 in

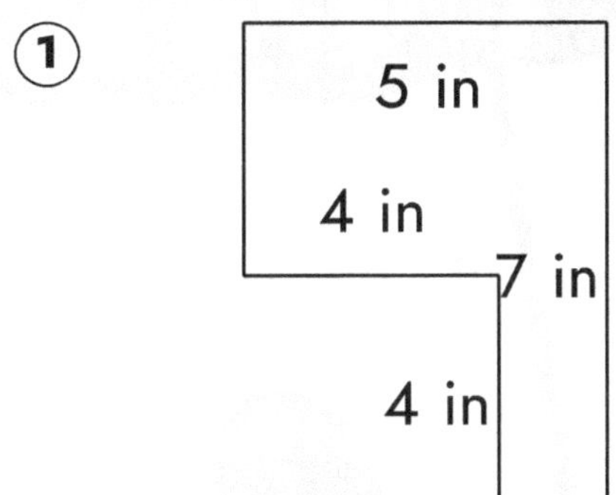

①

5 in
4 in
7 in
4 in

⑫

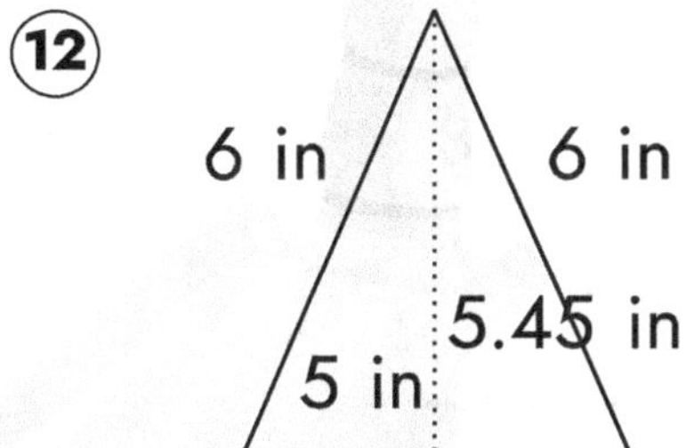

SUMMER MATH WORKBOOK
NAME:
BUILDING ACTIVITIES

13

10 in
10 in
8.660 in
10 in

14

6 in
2 in
7 in
3 in

15

8 in
8 in
6.928 in
8 in

16

10 in
7 in
9 in
5 in

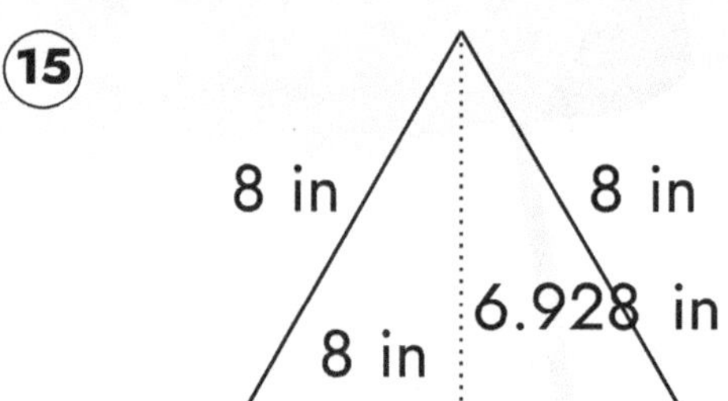

(17)

10 in
10 in
9 in

(1)

5 in
10 in
5 in
11 in

(19)

5 in
8 in
3.80 in
10 in

(20)

6 in
15 in
4 in
14 in

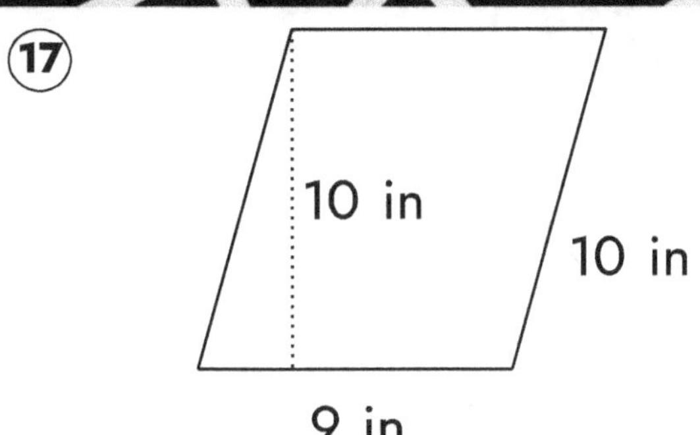

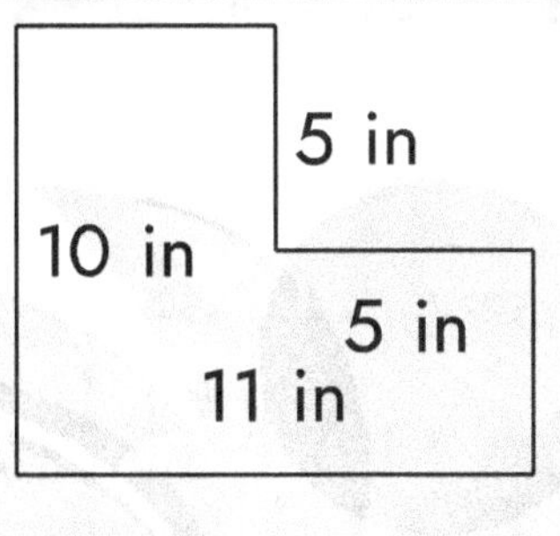

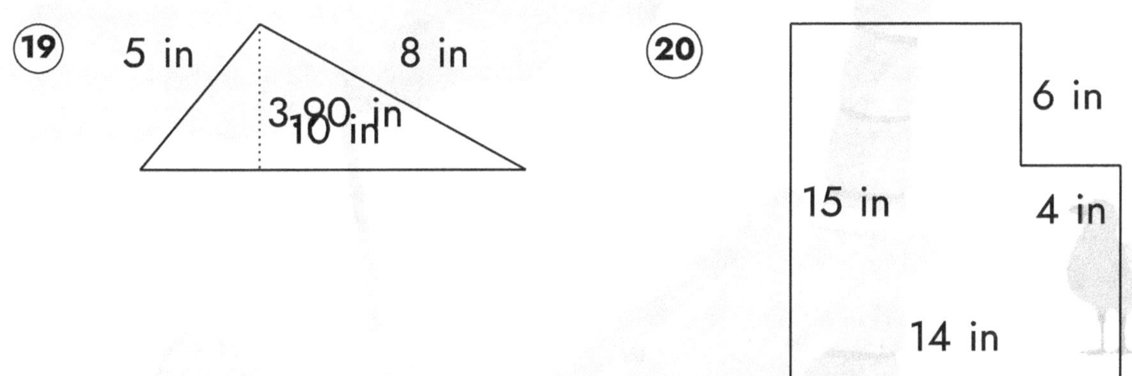

SUMMER MATH WORKBOOK
NAME:
BUILDING ACTIVITIES

(21)

5 in
11 in
5 in
8 in

(22)

12 in
12 in
10.392 in
12 in

(23)

10 in
10 in
5 in

(24)

14 in
8 in
5 in
5 in

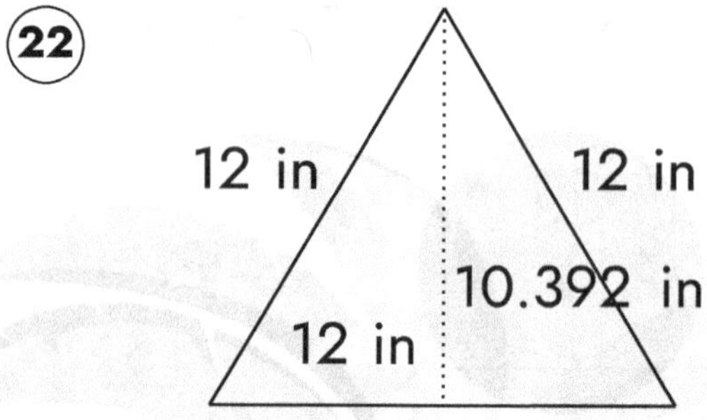

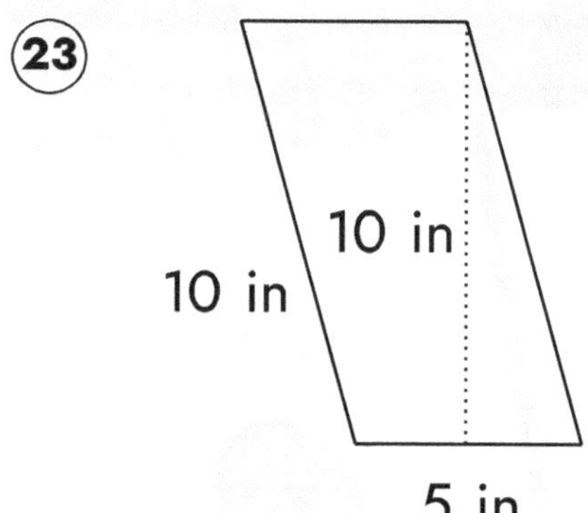

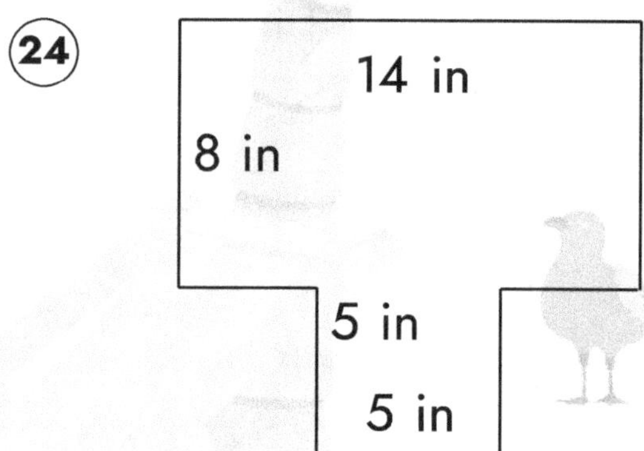

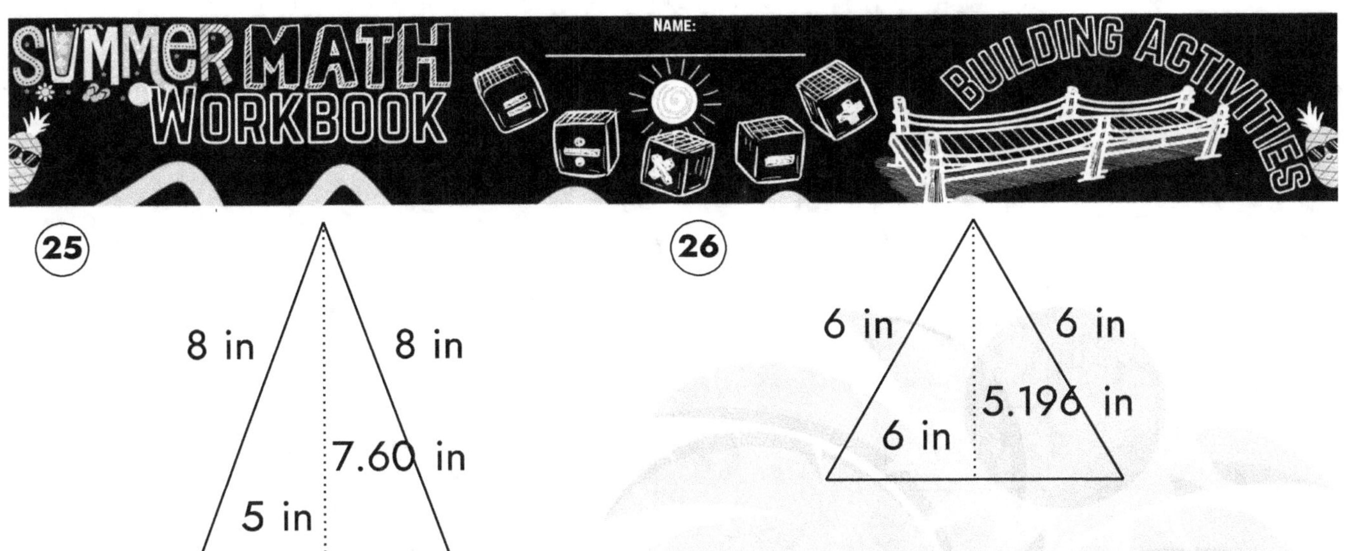
25
8 in
8 in
7.60 in
5 in
26
6 in
6 in
5.196 in
6 in

27
13 in
12 in
12 in
13 in
8 in
28
3 in
6 in
3 in
6 in

29

8 in
12 in
12 in 7 in

30

10 in   10 in
9.60 in
3 in

31

15 in   16 in
14.94 in
7 in

32

9 in
4 in
4 in
3 in

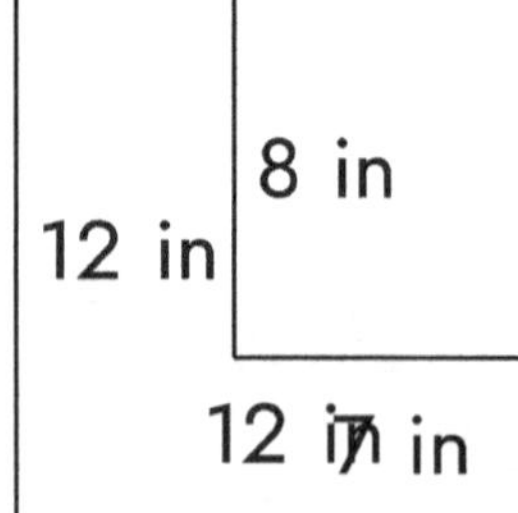

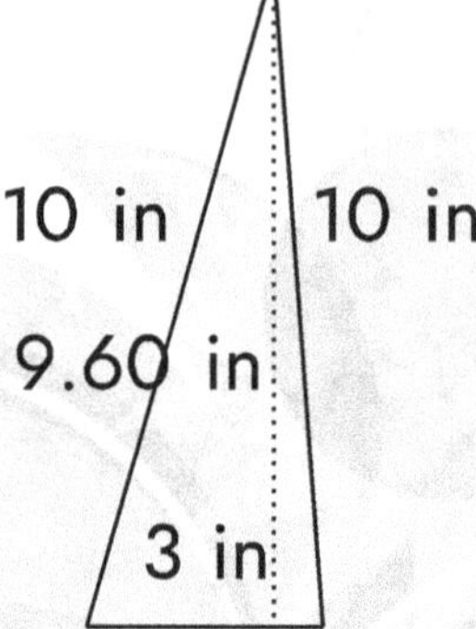

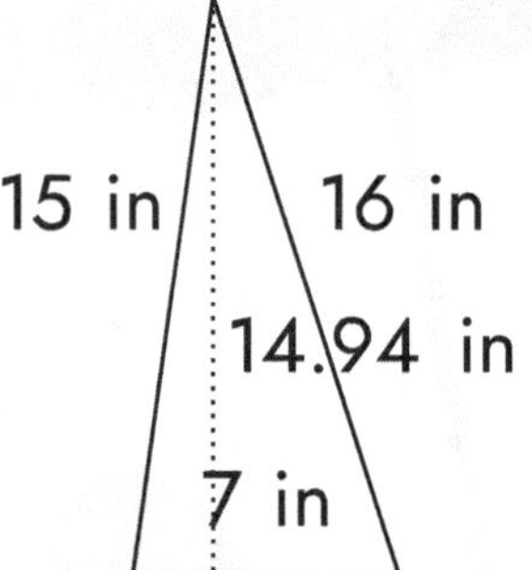

SUMMER MATH WORKBOOK
NAME:
BUILDING ACTIVITIES

(33)

5 in
7 in
8 in
5 in

(34)

8 in
12 in
11 in
11 in
15 in

(35)

15 in
15 in
13.96 in
11 in

(36)

10 in
6 in
5.04 in
11 in

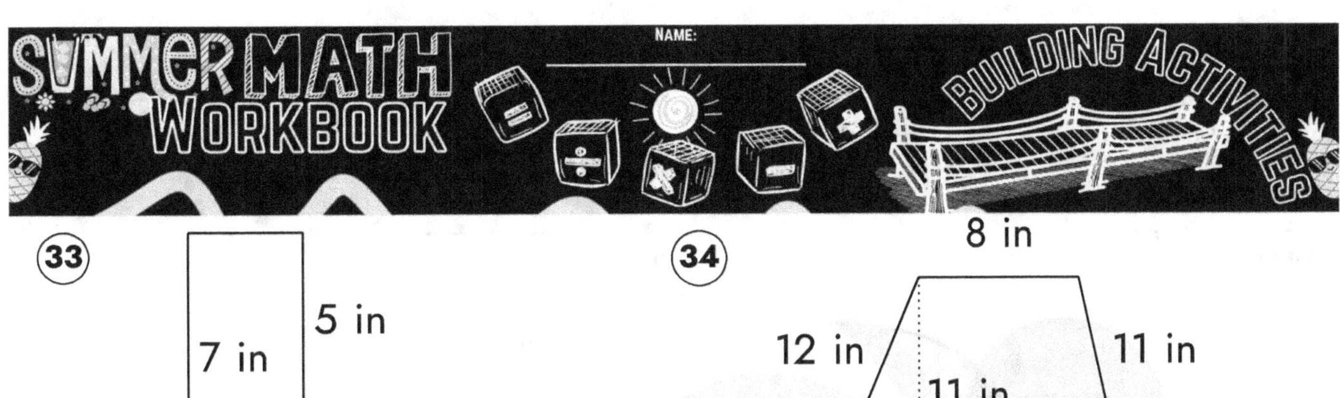

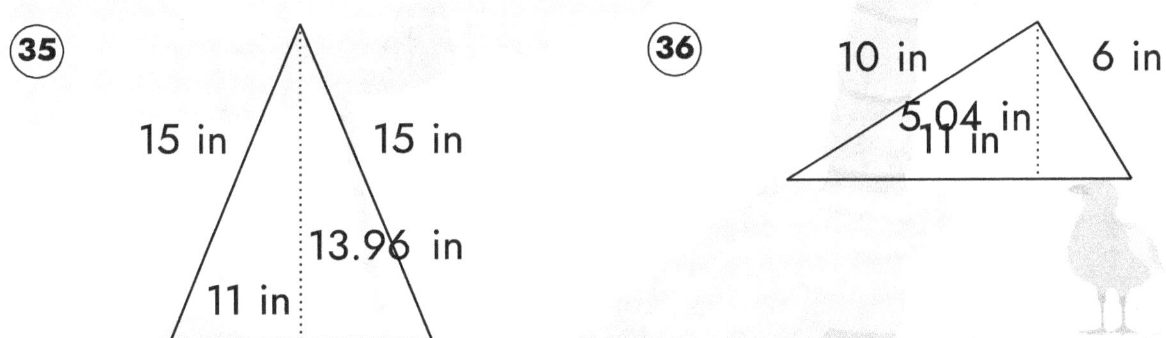

(37)

8 in
16 in 8 in
13 in

(38)

10 in
5 in
2 in
4 in

(39)

8 in
8 in
6.928 in
8 in

(40)

9 in
15 in
7 in
17 in

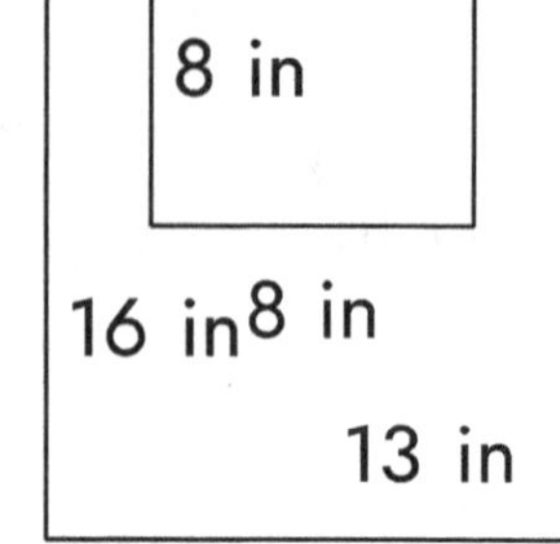

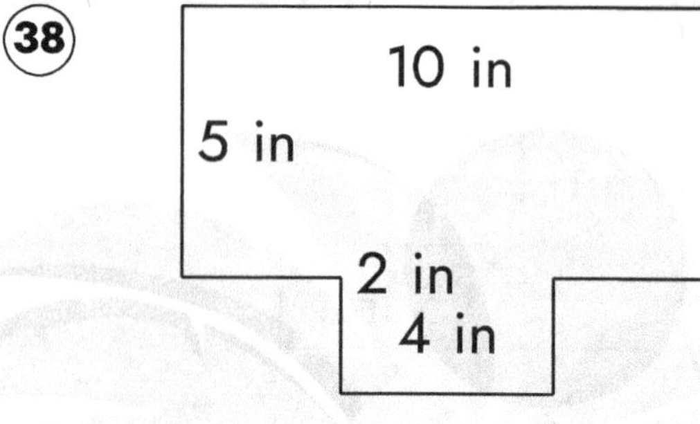

Volume and Surface Area

① 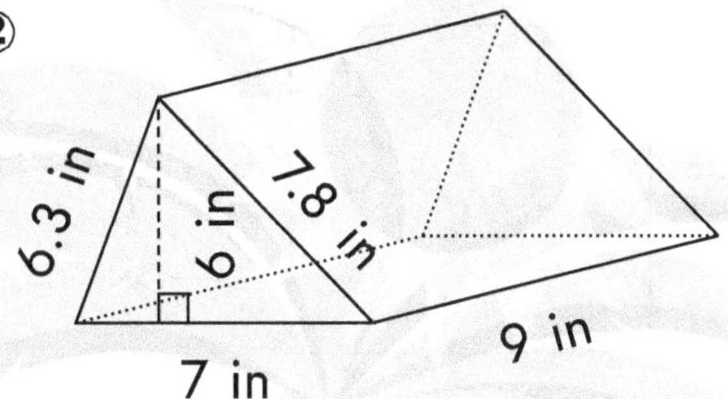

②

③ 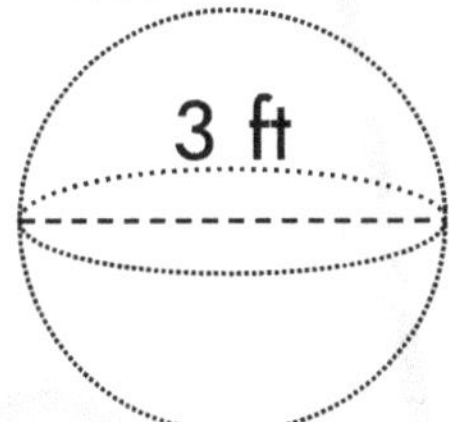

④ 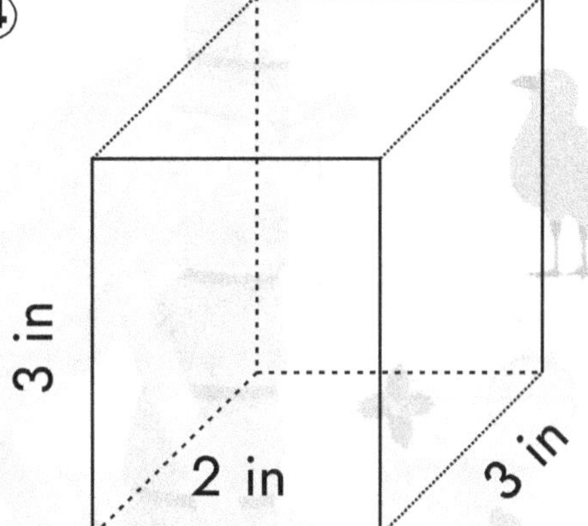

⑤ 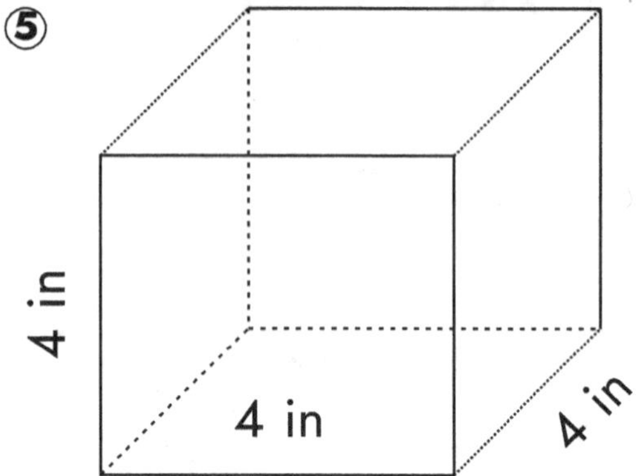

⑥ 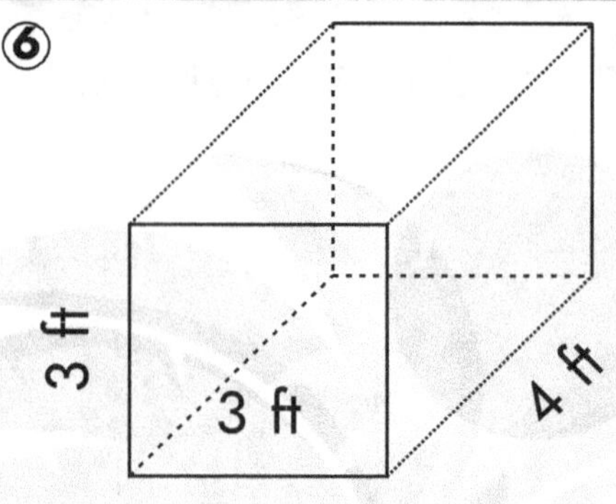

⑦ 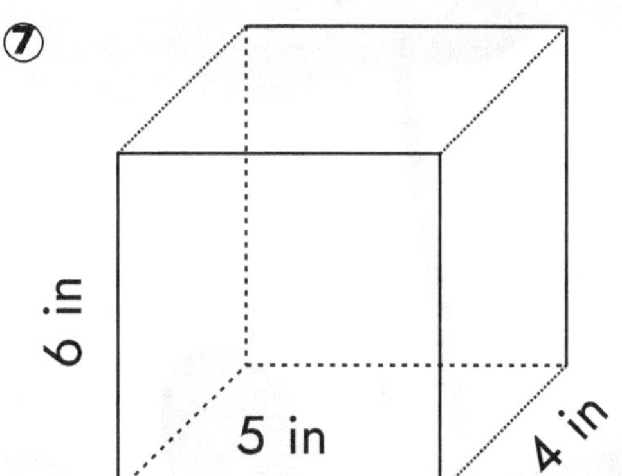

⑧ 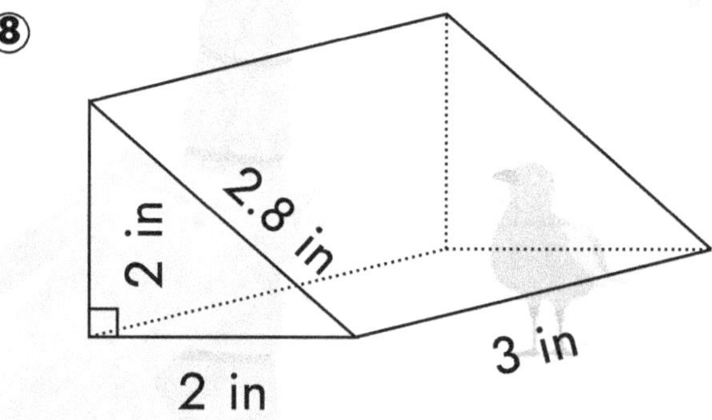

SUMMER MATH WORKBOOK
NAME:
BUILDING ACTIVITIES

⑨

2 in
3 in

⑩

7.8 cm
6 cm
5 cm
4 cm

①

8.1 ft
8.1 ft
7 ft
8 ft
9 ft

⑫

4 ft
6 ft

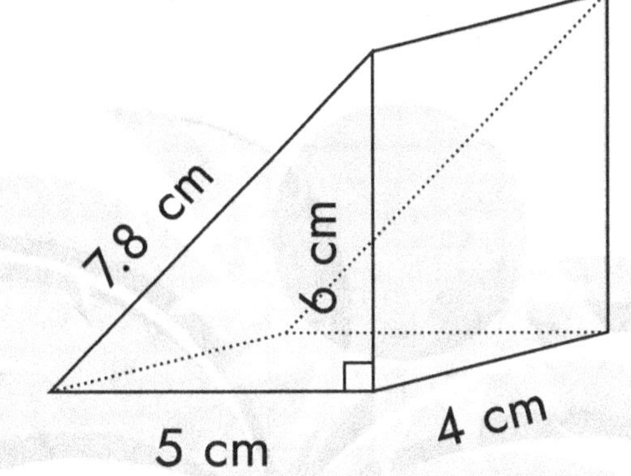

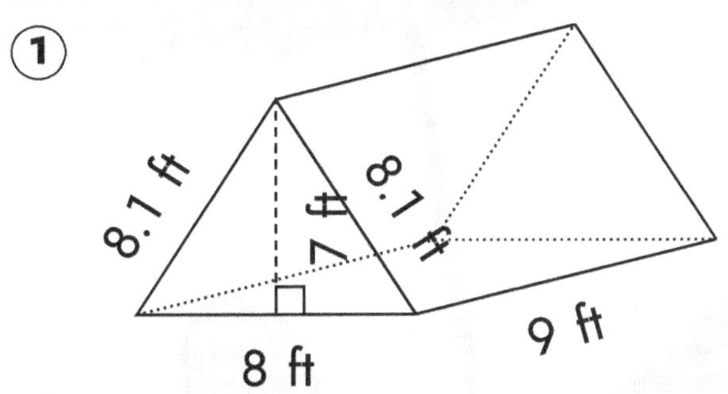

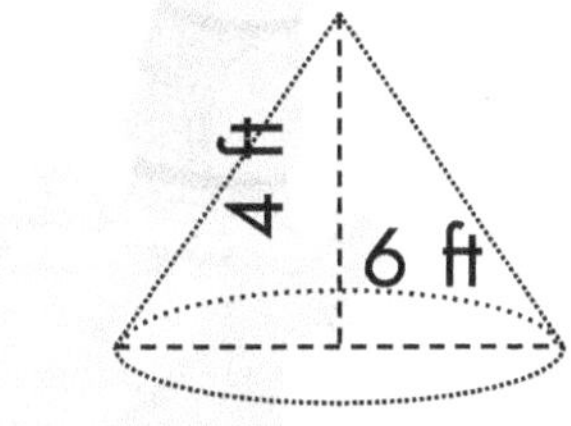

SUMMER MATH WORKBOOK
NAME:
BUILDING ACTIVITIES

(13)

6 in
7 in
6 in

(14)

6 ft
4 ft

(15)

7 ft
6 ft

(16)

7 ft
9 ft
8 ft

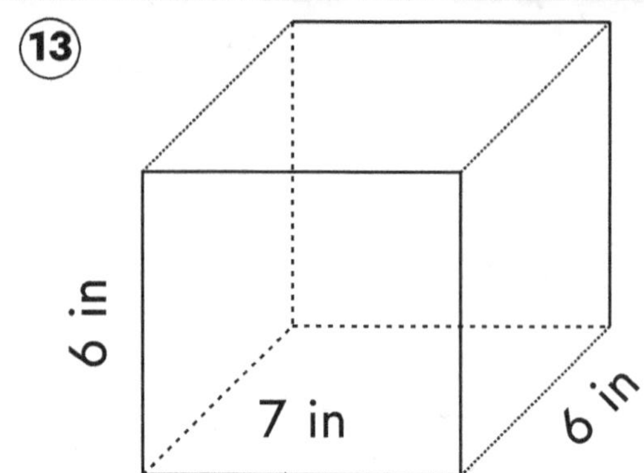

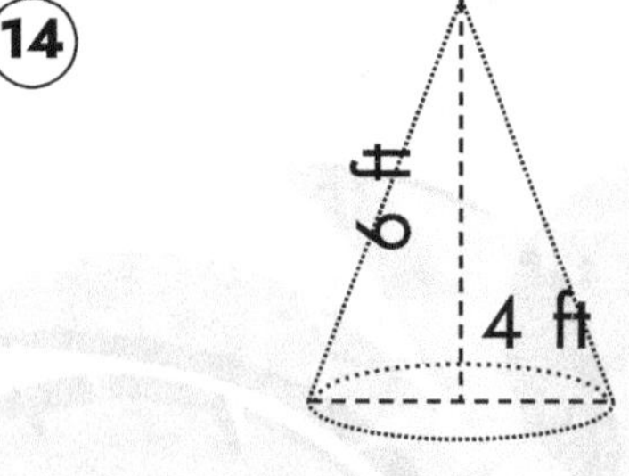

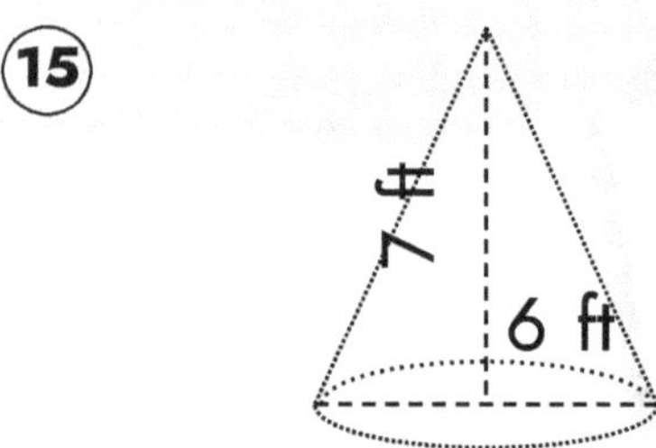

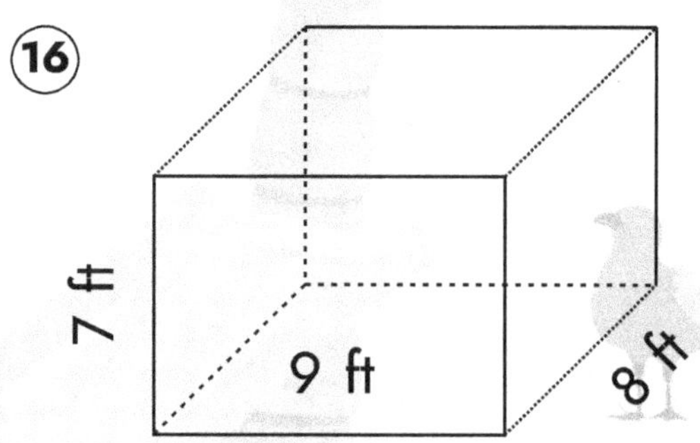

17

6 ft
5 ft
6 ft

1

4.1 cm
4 cm
5.7 cm
5 cm
5 cm

19

6 cm
4 cm
7 cm

20

7.6 ft
7 ft
7.6 ft
6 ft
8 ft

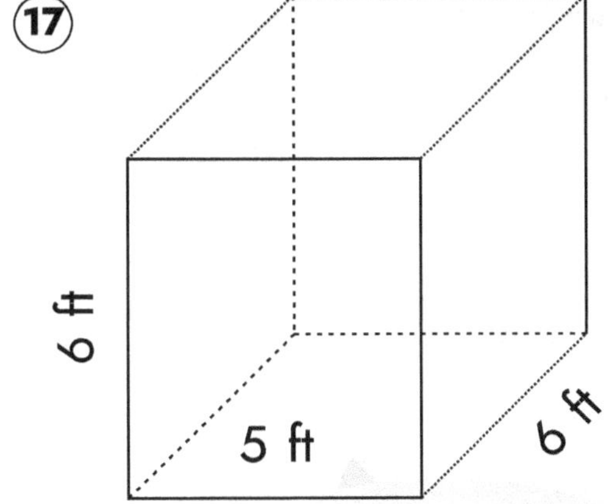

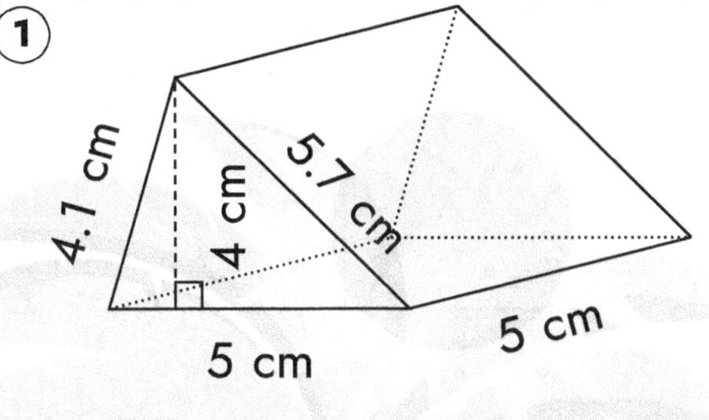

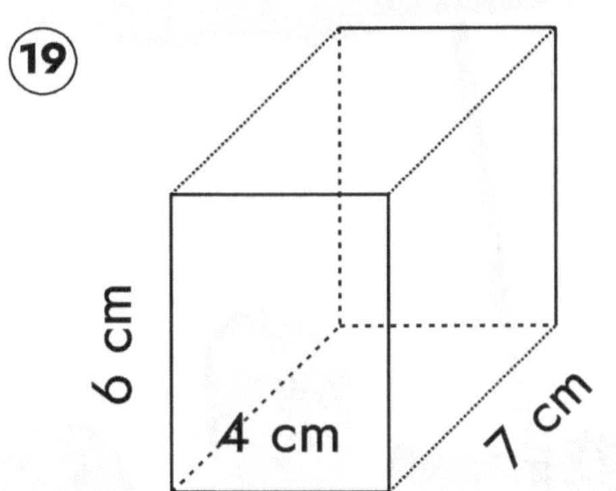

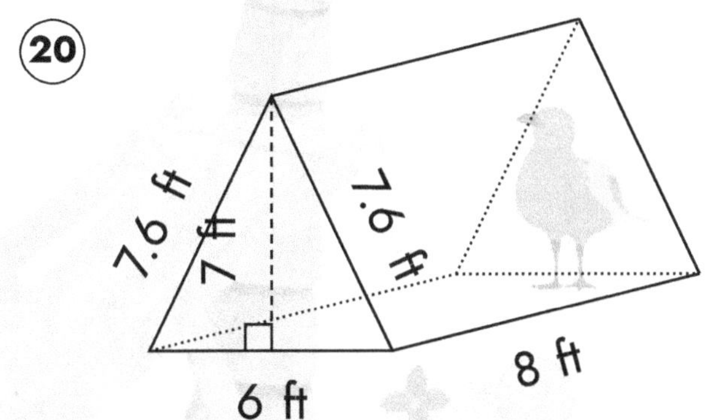

21

22

23

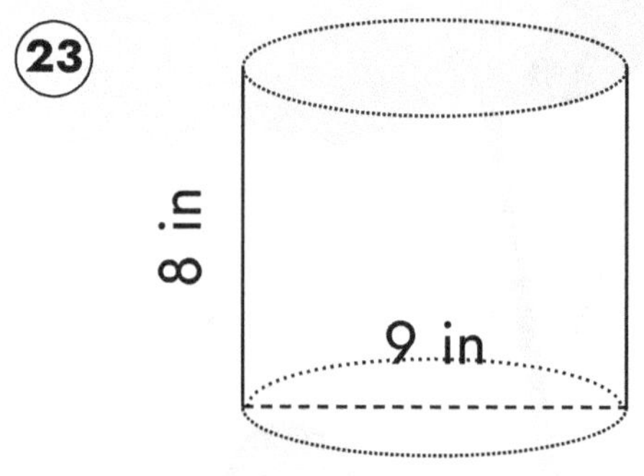

24

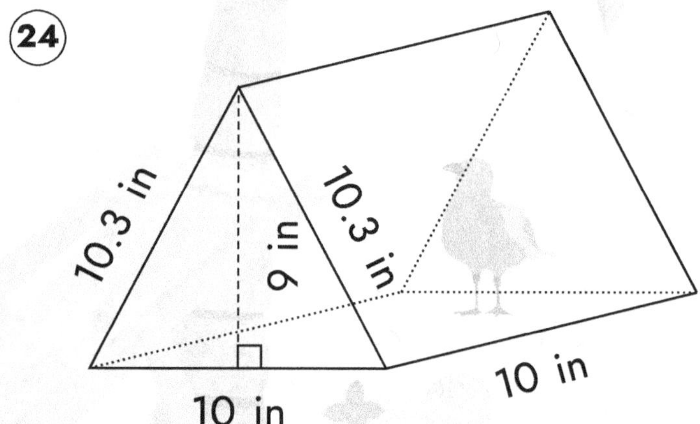

SUMMER MATH WORKBOOK
NAME:
BUILDING ACTIVITIES

25

2 cm
2 cm
3 cm

26

5 cm
8 cm

27

10 ft

28

3 cm
2 cm
3 cm

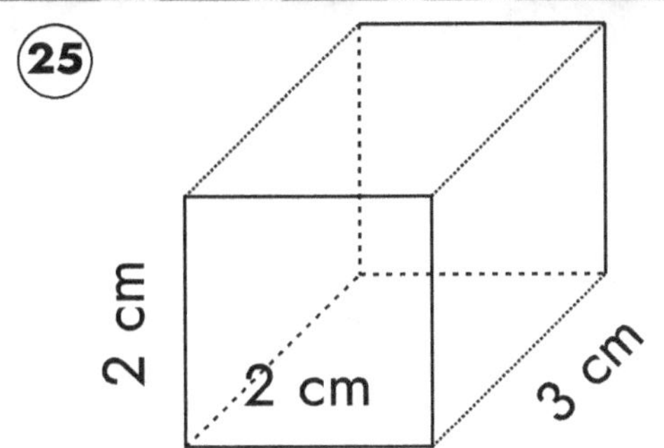

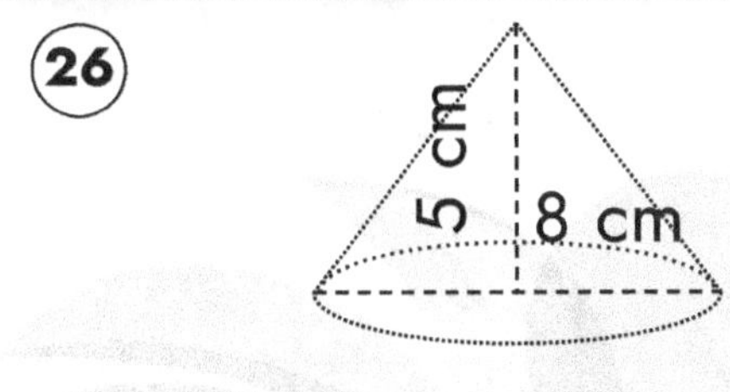

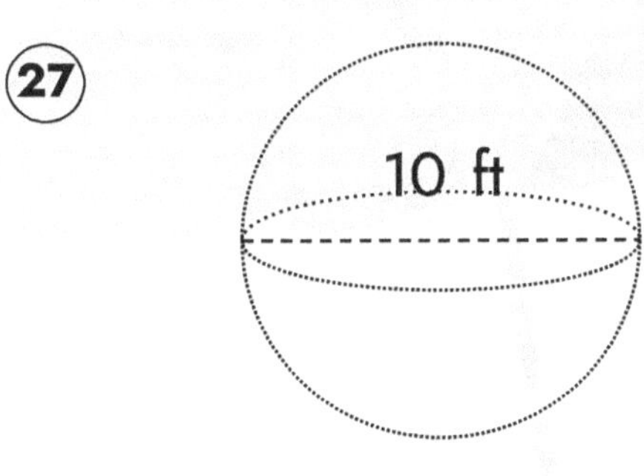

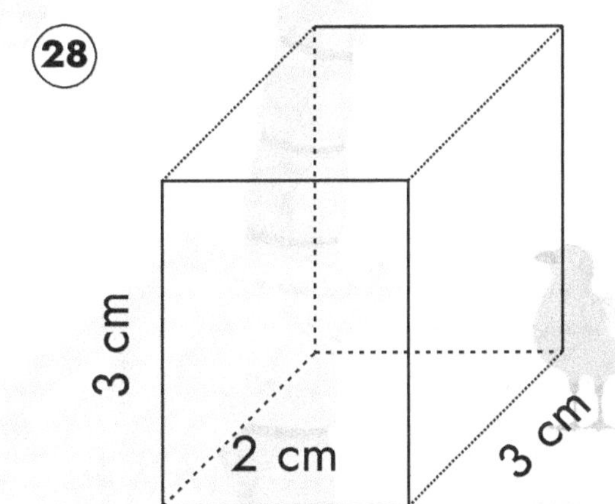

Pythagorean Theorem

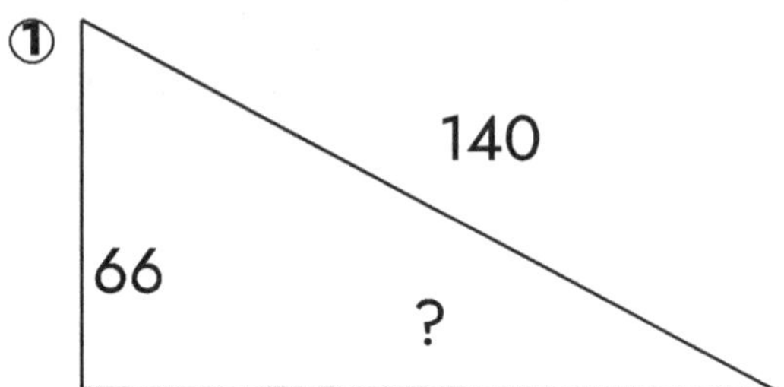

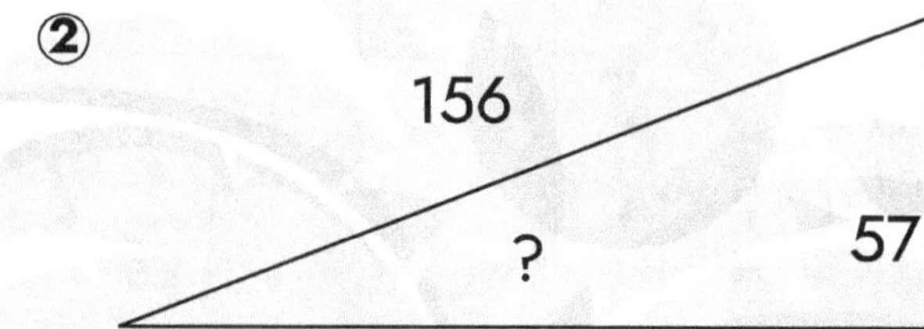

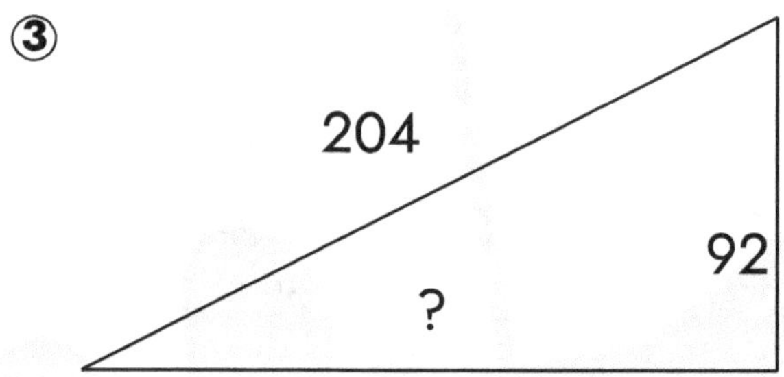

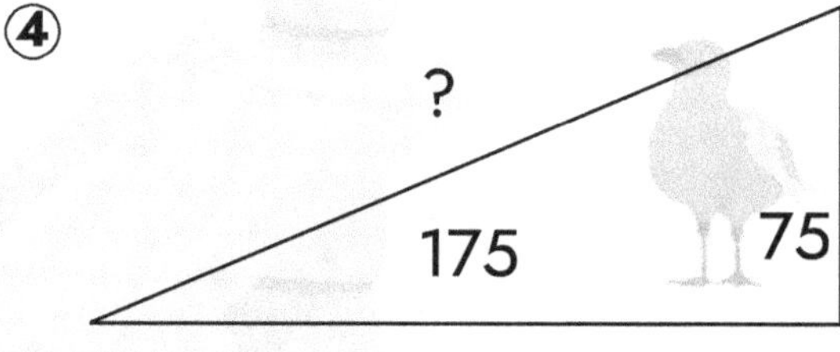

⑤ 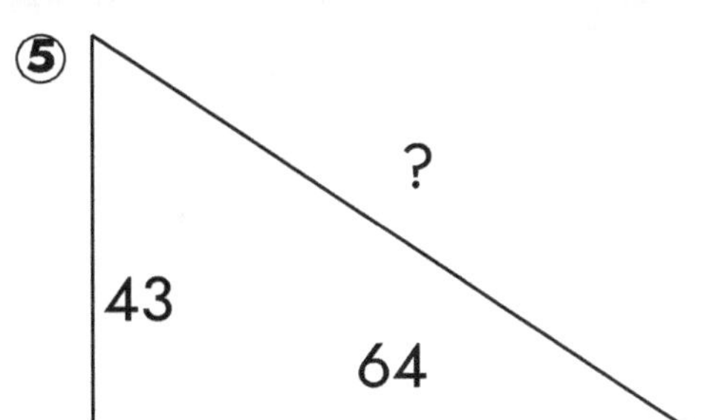

43

?

64

⑥ 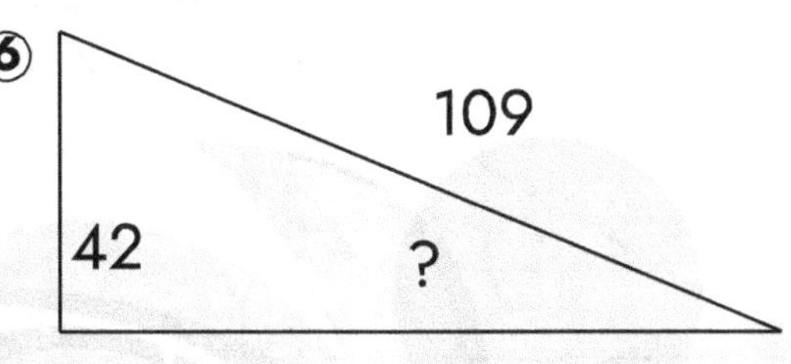

109

42

?

⑦ 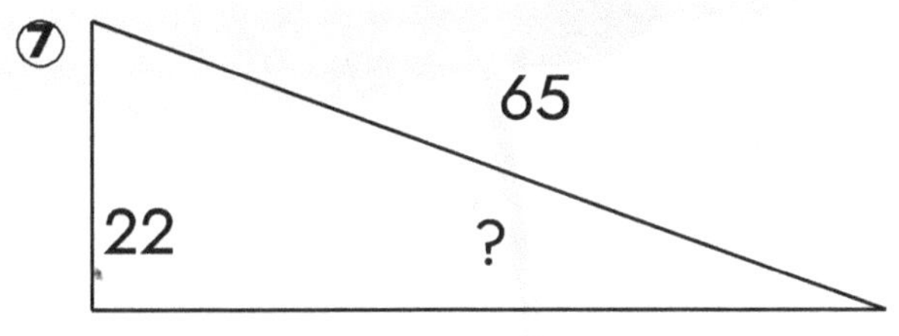

65

22

?

⑧ 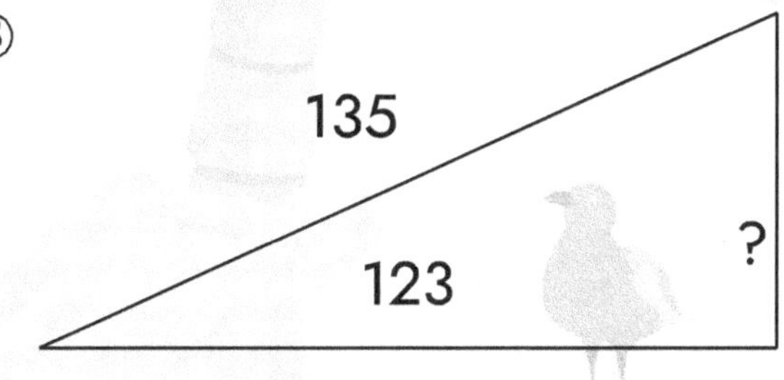

135

123

?

SUMMER MATH WORKBOOK
NAME:
BUILDING ACTIVITIES

⑨

181
157
?

⑩

?
68
31

①

80
?
67

⑫

237
?
211

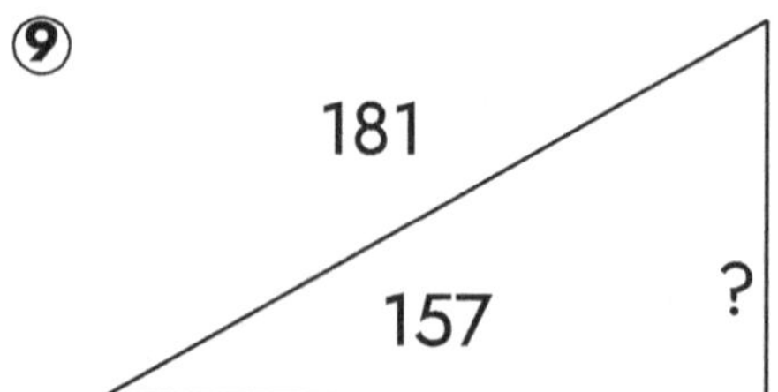

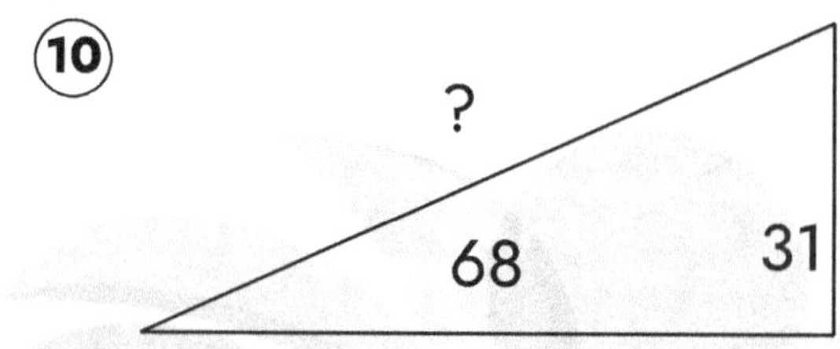

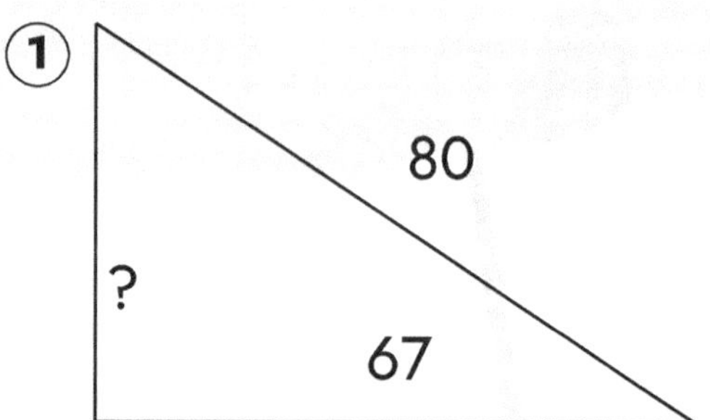

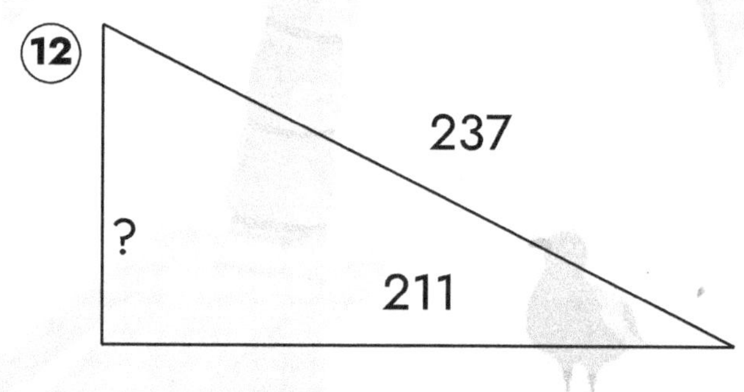

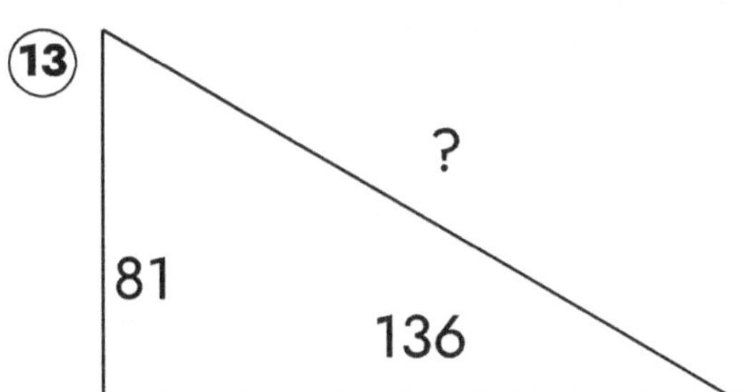

13
?
81
136

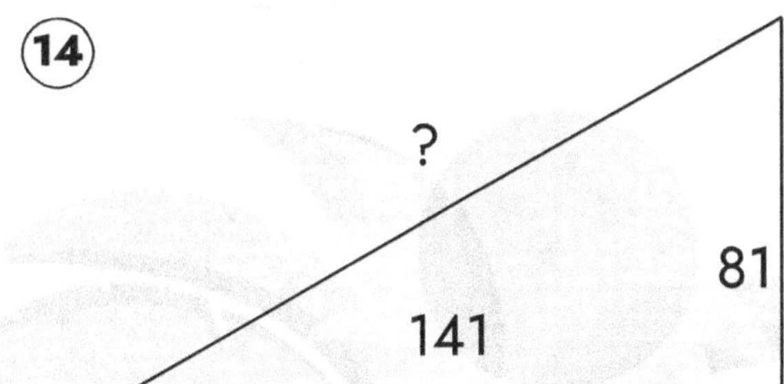

14
?
81
141

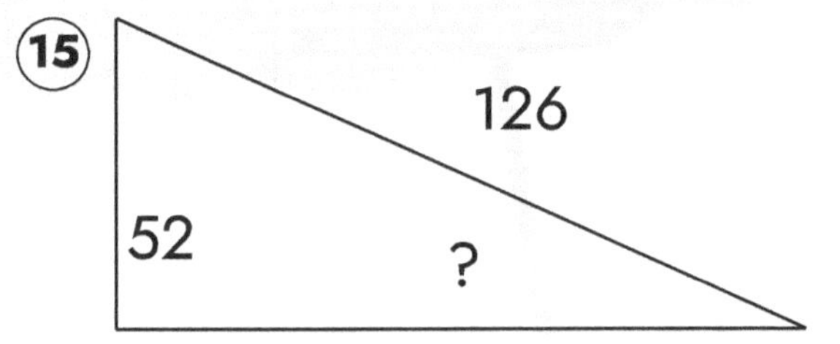

15
126
52
?

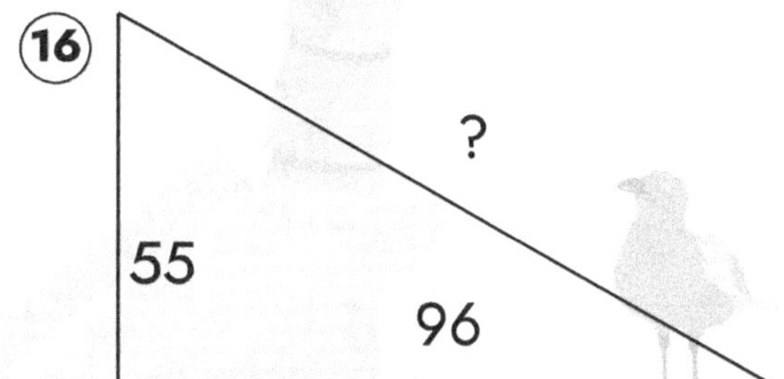

16
?
55
96

17

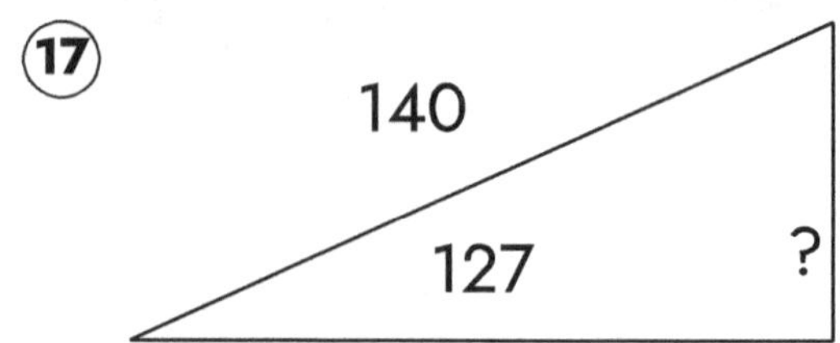

1

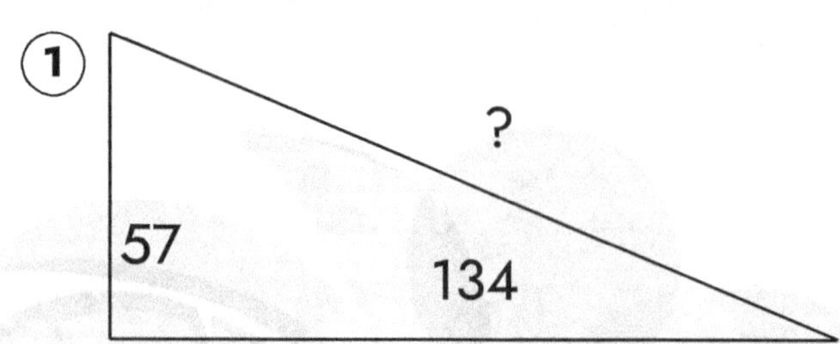

19

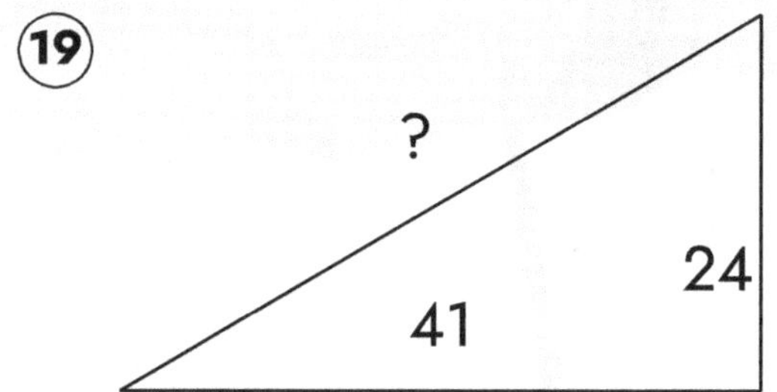

20

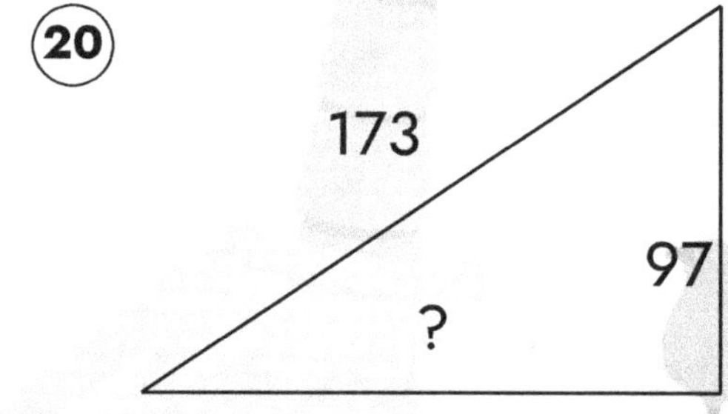

ANSWERS

Page 1:   Equations (Two Sides)

1. y = 3   **2.** z = 8   **3.** k = 2   **4.** x = 1   **5.** k = 9   **6.** z = 2   **7.** k = 7

8. z = 7   **9.** y = 7   **10.** k = 4   **11.** x = 2   **12.** x = 6   **13.** y = 5   **14.** x = 5

15. y = 6   **16.** k = 4   **17.** m = 2   **18.** y = 3   **19.** m = 6   **20.** y = 6   **21.** x = 7

22. y = 7   **23.** x = 3   **24.** z = 8   **25.** x = 7   **26.** x = 1   **27.** y = 1   **28.** y = 1

29. m = 8

Page 7:   Simplify Expressions

1. 5m + 7   **2.** y + 9   **3.** 12k + 9   **4.** –5y + 37   **5.** –14k + 6

6. –3y – 1   **7.** –9z   **8.** 2k – 6   **9.** 6z + 8   **10.** 36z – 65

11. –6m + 29   **12.** 6x – 11   **13.** 7   **14.** 5y   **15.** 9m + 12

16. –10y + 17   **17.** 3m + 1   **18.** -2   **19.** 10x – 5   **20.** 7x + 7

21. –13z – 7   **22.** –6y + 6   **23.** 2k + 8   **24.** 9k + 1   **25.** 3k + 13

26. 3k – 10   **27.** 21k – 3   **28.** 8z   **29.** –2x + 3

Page 13:   Order of Operations (PEMDAS)

1. 140   **2.** 19   **3.** 1,607   **4.** 23   **5.** 19   **6.** 30

7. 18   **8.** 117   **9.** 54   **10.** 90   **11.** 8,108   **12.** 29

13. 8   **14.** 29   **15.** 24   **16.** 40   **17.** 110   **18.** 1

19. 75   **20.** 57   **21.** 90   **22.** 198   **23.** 24   **24.** 4,909

25. -9   **26.** 70   **27.** 81   **28.** 64

Page 16:   Simplifying Equations

1. 14   **2.** 3   **3.** -5   **4.** 13   **5.** -6   **6.** 11   **7.** -1   **8.** 4

Page 17:   Simplifying Equations

1. -20   **2.** -1   **3.** -8   **4.** -9   **5.** -16   **6.** 9   **7.** 19   **8.** -6

Page 18:   Simplifying Equations

1. -16   **2.** -4   **3.** 4   **4.** -14   **5.** 19   **6.** -3   **7.** -12   **8.** -1

Page 19:   Simplifying Equations

1. -10   **2.** 5   **3.** 15   **4.** -17   **5.** -12   **6.** 1   **7.** -14   **8.** -2

Page 20:   Solving Inequalities

1. $m < 0$ **2.** $z \geq 10$ **3.** $y < -3$ **4.** $m \leq -6/5$ **5.** $y < -10$ **6.** $y > -3/7$

7. $z > -9$ **8.** $k \geq 5$ **9.** $x \leq -1$ **10.** $k > 12$ **11.** $y \leq 5/4$ **12.** $y \leq -4$

13. $z > -12$ **14.** $z \leq -6$ **15.** $m < 4$ **16.** $k \leq 30$ **17.** $y \leq 17$ **18.** $k > -6/5$

19. $m > 10$ **20.** $k > 16$ **21.** $y < -8$ **22.** $x \leq -1$ **23.** $m \geq 12$ **24.** $y > -2$

Page 26: Linear Equations

1. 9	**8.** 3	**15.** 2
2. 10	**9.** -9	**16.** -2
3. 1	**10.** 8	**17.** -10
4. -3	**11.** -6	**18.** -3
5. -8	**12.** 7	**19.** 10
6. -4	**13.** 1	**20.** 3
7. 1	**14.** -5	

Page 29: System of Equations

1. x = -0.36, y = 0.39
2. x = 2.25, y = -1.25
3. x = -3.5, y = 6.5
4. x = 0.5, y = 0.75
5. x = 0.27, y = 0.83
6. x = 0.29, y = 0.15
7. x = 0.38, y = -0.04
8. x = -3.0, y = 19.0
9. x = -5.0, y = 4.0
10. x = 0.1, y = 1.2
11. x = 0.56, y = 0.08
12. x = 0.25, y = 0.25

Page 33: Verbal Algebra Expressions

1. 2	2. 3	3. 4, 6	4. 4, 6, 8	5. 5, 6, 7
6. 10	7. 5, 25	8. 9, 18	9. 6, 7, 8	10. 9, 54
11. 8	12. 4	13. 25	14. 5	15. 8, 5
16. 6	17. 6	18. 13, 4	19. 7, 8, 9, 10	20. 12
21. 3, 4	22. 13, 3	23. 3, 21	24. 4, 2	25. 8

Page 39:   Percent

1. 3.6%	2. 0.396	3. 0.5%	4. 0.8%	5. 2	6. 17.8%
7. 3	8. 0.4%	9. 83.16	10. 19	11. 34.8%	12. 0.5%
13. 3.1%	14. 407	15. 0.048	16. 19.074	17. 0.462	18. 0.4%
19. 0.6%	20. 0.312	21. 17.86	22. 1.72	23. 0.2%	24. 77
25. 9.2%	26. 0.105	27. 6.9%	28. 1.029		

Page 42: Convert: Ratio, Fraction, Percent, and Decimals

1.

	Ratio	Fraction	Percent	Decimal
a.	2:20	2/20	10%	0.1
b.	4:15	4/15	26.7%	0.267
c.	1:1	1/1	100%	1
d.	6:7	6/7	85.7%	0.857
e.	3:7	3/7	42.9%	0.429
f.	7:13	7/13	53.8%	0.538
g.	1:6	1/6	16.7%	0.167
h.	3:14	3/14	21.4%	0.214
i.	2:5	2/5	40%	0.4
j.	2:9	2/9	22.2%	0.222
k.	17:19	17/19	89.5%	0.895
l.	2:8	2/8	25%	0.25
m.	5:12	5/12	41.7%	0.417
n.	9:14	9/14	64.3%	0.643
o.	2:3	2/3	66.7%	0.667

2.

	Ratio	Fraction	Percent	Decimal
a.	6:7	6/7	85.7%	0.857
b.	2:15	2/15	13.3%	0.133
c.	1:2	1/2	50%	0.5
d.	1:16	1/16	6.2%	0.062
e.	1:14	1/14	7.1%	0.071
f.	19:20	19/20	95%	0.95
g.	1:3	1/3	33.3%	0.333
h.	3:11	3/11	27.3%	0.273
i.	13:15	13/15	86.7%	0.867
j.	9:10	9/10	90%	0.9
k.	3:3	3/3	100%	1
l.	16:18	16/18	88.9%	0.889
m.	2:8	2/8	25%	0.25
n.	5:6	5/6	83.3%	0.833
o.	6:14	6/14	42.9%	0.429

3.

	Ratio	Fraction	Percent	Decimal
a.	6:6	6/6	100%	1
b.	2:4	2/4	50%	0.5
c.	5:7	5/7	71.4%	0.714
d.	5:10	5/10	50%	0.5
e.	8:18	8/18	44.4%	0.444
f.	1:2	1/2	50%	0.5
g.	9:18	9/18	50%	0.5
h.	6:17	6/17	35.3%	0.353
i.	3:9	3/9	33.3%	0.333
j.	4:7	4/7	57.1%	0.571
k.	14:15	14/15	93.3%	0.933
l.	1:5	1/5	20%	0.2
m.	11:18	11/18	61.1%	0.611
n.	2:14	2/14	14.3%	0.143
o.	3:18	3/18	16.7%	0.167

4.

	Ratio	Fraction	Percent	Decimal
a.	8:15	8/15	53.3%	0.533
b.	9:9	9/9	100%	1
c.	2:8	2/8	25%	0.25
d.	9:20	9/20	45%	0.45
e.	1:17	1/17	5.9%	0.059
f.	6:7	6/7	85.7%	0.857
g.	7:18	7/18	38.9%	0.389
h.	9:13	9/13	69.2%	0.692
i.	7:16	7/16	43.8%	0.438
j.	7:13	7/13	53.8%	0.538
k.	4:11	4/11	36.4%	0.364
l.	15:16	15/16	93.8%	0.938
m.	7:8	7/8	87.5%	0.875
n.	9:12	9/12	75%	0.75
o.	11:12	11/12	91.7%	0.917

5.

	Ratio	Fraction	Percent	Decimal
a.	8:17	8/17	47.1%	0.471
b.	2:3	2/3	66.7%	0.667
c.	15:19	15/19	78.9%	0.789
d.	8:8	8/8	100%	1
e.	7:11	7/11	63.6%	0.636
f.	4:11	4/11	36.4%	0.364
g.	4:7	4/7	57.1%	0.571
h.	13:16	13/16	81.2%	0.812
i.	5:10	5/10	50%	0.5
j.	9:14	9/14	64.3%	0.643
k.	12:13	12/13	92.3%	0.923
l.	8:14	8/14	57.1%	0.571
m.	2:6	2/6	33.3%	0.333
n.	3:16	3/16	18.8%	0.188
o.	2:5	2/5	40%	0.4

Page 47: Plotting Lines

1.

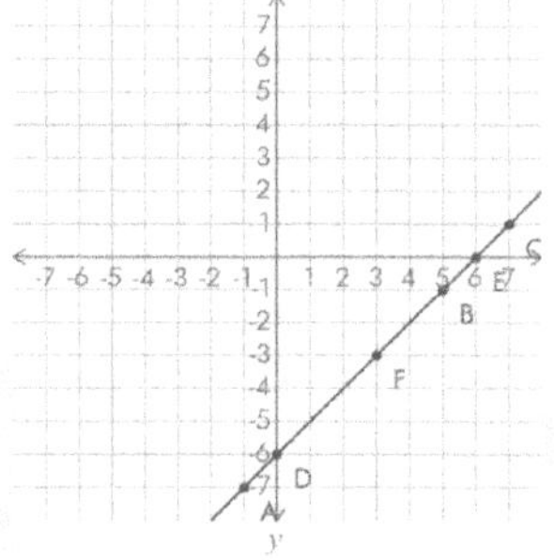

A = (-1, -7)   B = (5, -1)

C = (7, 1)   D = (0, -6)

E = (6, 0)   F = (3, -3)

2.

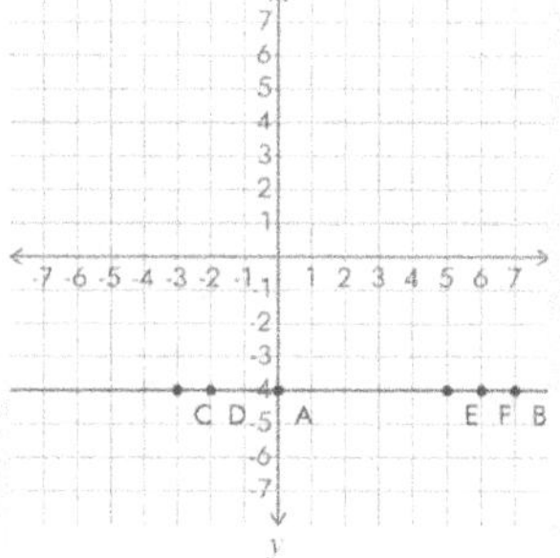

A = (0, -4)   B = (7, -4)

C = (-3, -4)   D = (-2, -4)

E = (5, -4)   F = (6, -4)

3.

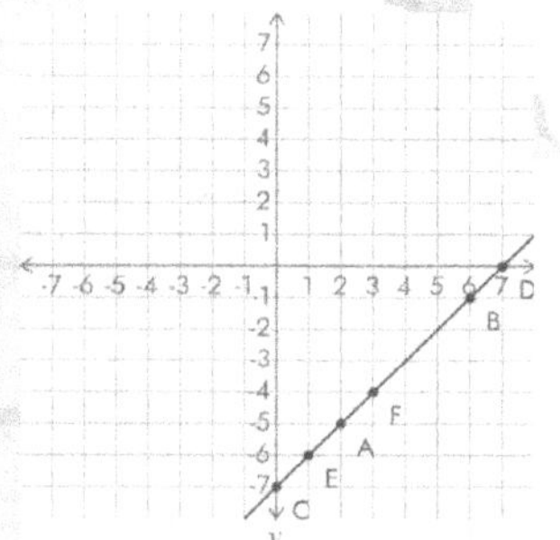

A = (2, -5)   B = (6, -1)

C = (0, -7)   D = (7, 0)

E = (1, -6)   F = (3, -4)

4. 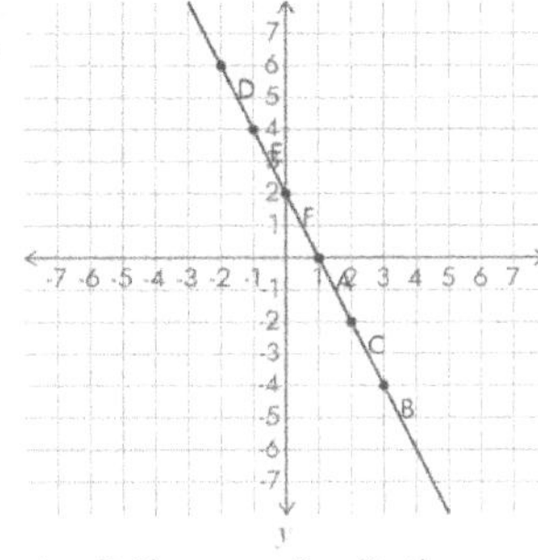

A = (1, 0)   B = (3, -4)

C = (2, -2)   D = (-2, 6)

E = (-1, 4)   F = (0, 2)

5. 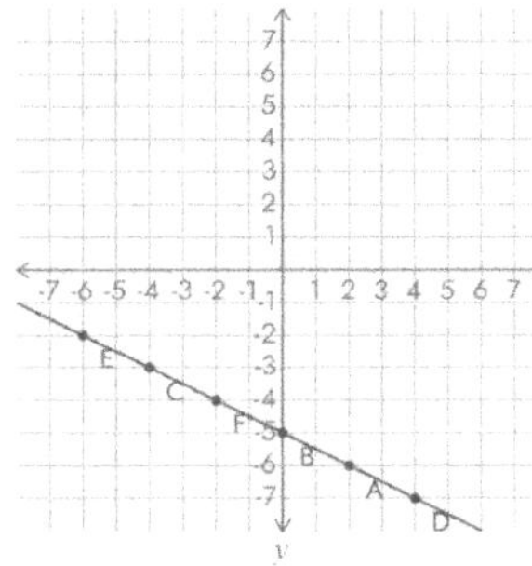

A = (2, -6)   B = (0, -5)

C = (-4, -3)   D = (4, -7)

E = (-6, -2)   F = (-2, -4)

Page 52:   Graphing Linear Equations

1. $y = \frac{-1}{2}x + 4$ 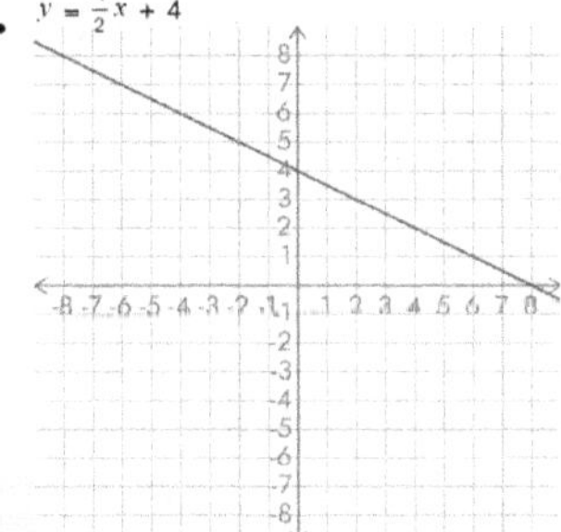

2. $y = \frac{-9}{4}x + 2$ 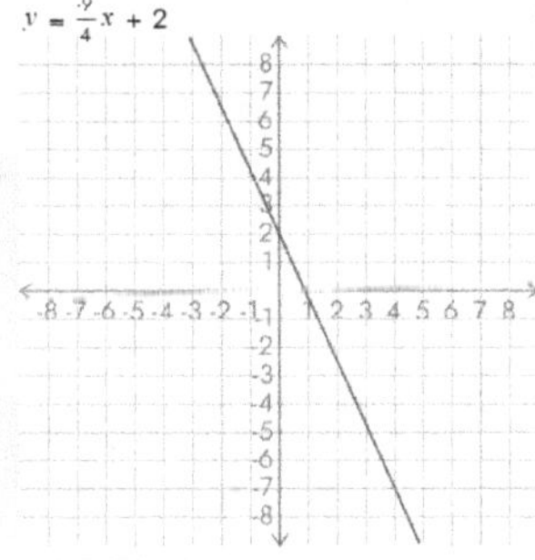

3. $y = \frac{5}{4}x + 6$ 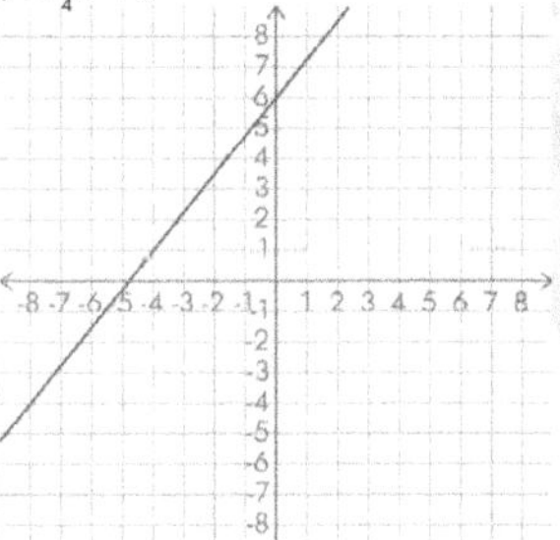

4. $y = \frac{7}{4}x - 2$ 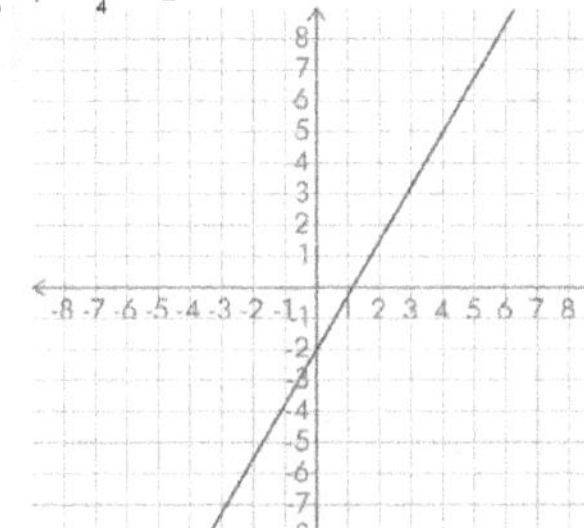

5. $y = \frac{-7}{4}x - 5$ 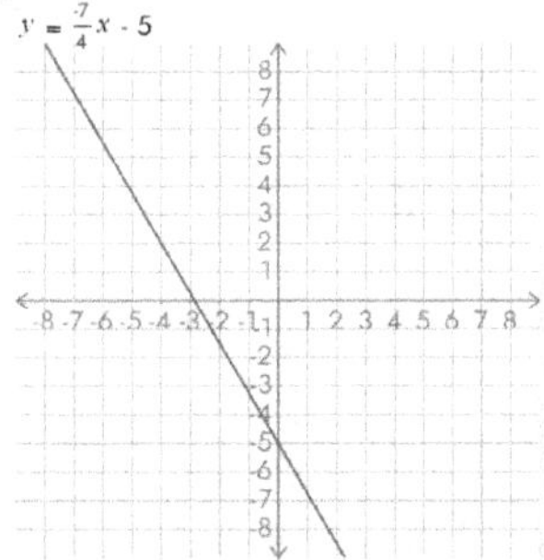

Page 57:   Cartesian Coordinates

1. 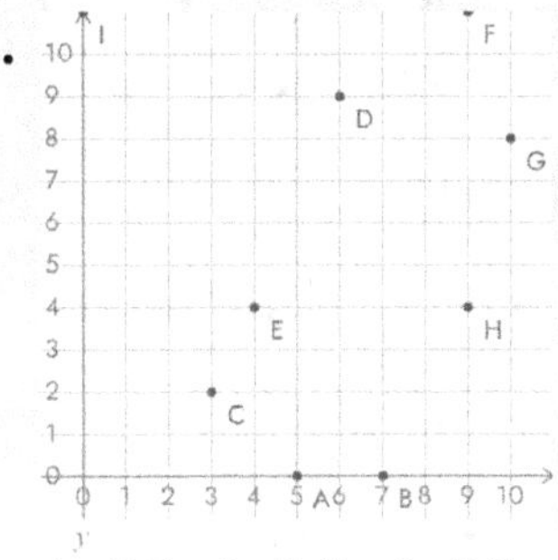

A = (5, 0)   B = (7, 0)   C = (3, 2)

D = (6, 9)   E = (4, 4)   F = (9, 10)

G = (10, 8)   H = (9, 4)   I = (0, 10)

2. 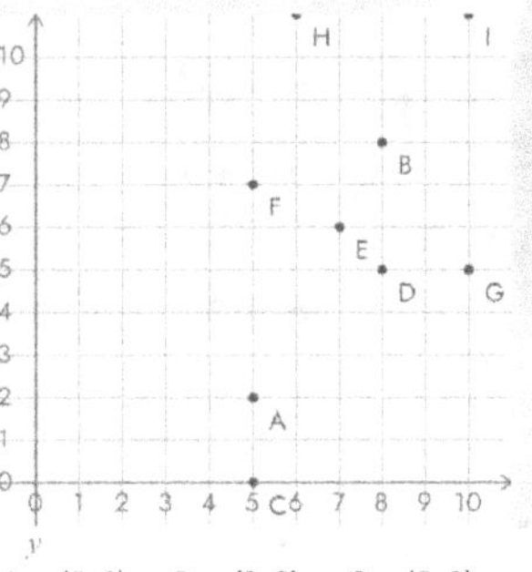

A = (5, 2)   B = (8, 8)   C = (5, 0)

D = (8, 5)   E = (7, 6)   F = (5, 7)

G = (10, 5)   H = (6, 10)   I = (10, 10)

3. 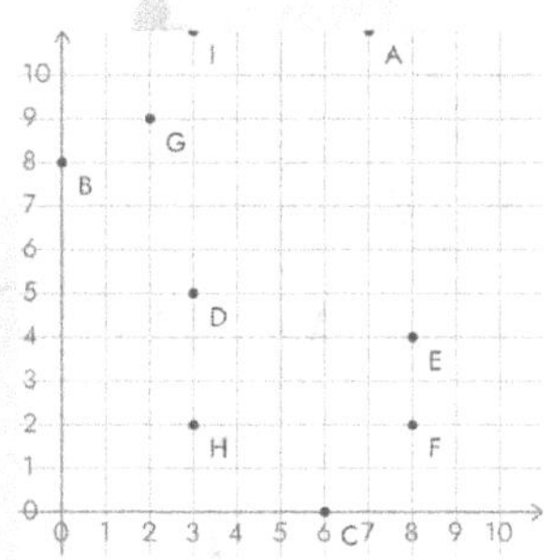

A = (7, 10)   B = (0, 8)   C = (6, 0)

D = (3, 5)   E = (8, 4)   F = (8, 2)

G = (2, 9)   H = (3, 2)   I = (3, 10)

Page 53:   Cartesian Coordinates

1. 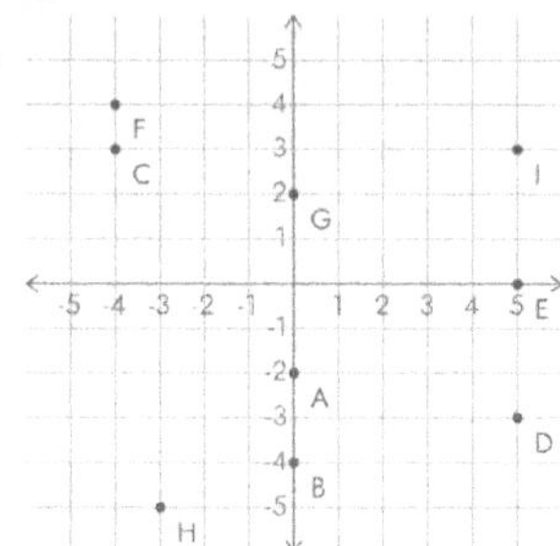

A = (0, -2)   B = (0, -4)   C = (-4, 3)

D = (5, -3)   E = (5, 0)   F = (-4, 4)

G = (0, 2)   H = (-3, -5)   I = (5, 3)

2. 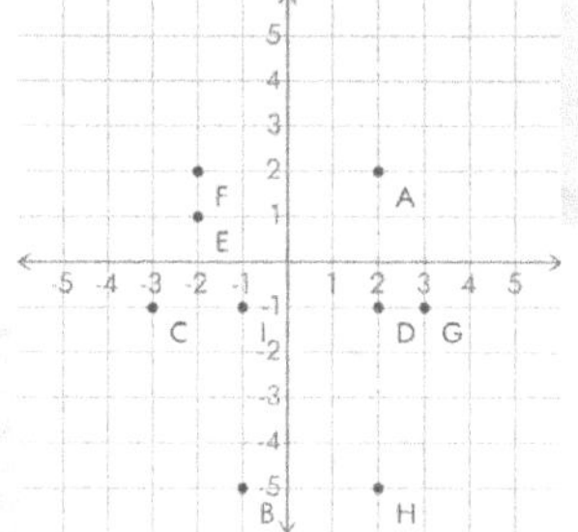

A = (2, 2)   B = (-1, -5)   C = (-3, -1)

D = (2, -1)   E = (-2, 1)   F = (-2, 2)

G = (3, -1)   H = (2, -5)   I = (-1, -1)

3. 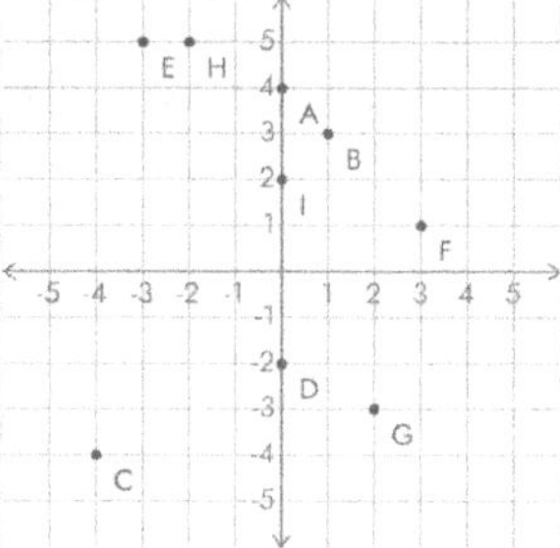

A = (0, 4)   B = (1, 3)   C = (-4, -4)

D = (0, -2)   E = (-3, 5)   F = (3, 1)

G = (2, -3)   H = (-2, 5)   I = (0, 2)

Page 63:   Area and Perimeter

1. P=62 A=144

2. P=50 A=111

3. P=24 A=27

4. P=43 A=55.08

5. P=20 A=21

6. P=19 A=11.34

7. P=37 A=81

8. P=26 A=35

9. P=48 A=108

10. P=28 A=49

11. P=24 A=19

12. P=17 A=13.62

13. P=30 A=43.3

14. P=26 A=36

15. P=24 A=27.71

16. P=38 A=55

17. P=38 A=90

18. P=42 A=85

19. P=23 A=19.5

20. P=58 A=186

21. P=38 A=63

22. P=36 A=62.35

23. P=30 A=50

24. P=54 A=137

25. P=21 A=19

26. P=18 A=15.59

27. P=46 A=126

28. P=24 A=27

29. P=48 A=88

30. P=23 A=14.4

31. P=38 A=52.29

32. P=34 A=48

33. P=30 A=31

34. P=46 A=126

35. P=41 A=76.78

36. P=27 A=27.72

37. P=74 A=144

38. P=34 A=58

39. P=24 A=27.71

40. P=82 A=192

Page 73: Volume and Surface Area

1. V=141.37 cm^3 cm^3 SA=151 cm^2 cm^2

2. V=189 in^3 in^3 SA=231.9 in^2 in^2

3. V=14 ft^3 ft^3 SA=28 ft^2 ft^2

4. V=18 in^3 in^3 SA=42 in^2 in^2

5. V=64 in^3 in^3 SA=96 in^2 in^2

6. V=36 ft^3 ft^3 SA=66 ft^2 ft^2

7. V=120 in^3 in^3 SA=148 in^2 in^2

8. V=6 in^3 in^3 SA=24.4 in^2 in^2

9. V=14.14 in^3 in^3 SA=33 in^2 in^2

10. V=60 cm^3 cm^3 SA=105.2 cm^2 cm^2

11. V=252 ft^3 ft^3 SA=273.8 ft^2 ft^2

12. V=38 ft^3 ft^3 SA=75 ft^2 ft^2

13. V=252 in^3 in^3 SA=240 in^2 in^2

14. V=25 ft^3 ft^3 SA=52 ft^2 ft^2

15. V=66 ft^3 ft^3 SA=100 ft^2 ft^2

16. V=504 ft^3 ft^3 SA=382 ft^2 ft^2

17. V=180 ft^3 ft^3 SA=192 ft^2 ft^2

18. V=50 cm^3 cm^3 SA=94.0 cm^2 cm^2

19. V=168 cm^3 cm^3 SA=188 cm^2 cm^2

20. V=168 ft^3 ft^3 SA=211.6 ft^2 ft^2

21. V=216 ft^3 ft^3 SA=264 ft^2 ft^2

22. V=58.90 ft^3 ft^3 SA=86 ft^2 ft^2

23. V=508.94 in^3 in^3 SA=353 in^2 in^2

24. V=450 in^3 in^3 SA=396.0 in^2 in^2

25. V=12 cm^3 cm^3 SA=32 cm^2 cm^2

26. V=84 cm^3 cm^3 SA=131 cm^2 cm^2

27. V=524 ft^3 ft^3 SA=314 ft^2 ft^2

28. V=18 cm^3 cm^3 SA=42 cm^2 cm^2

Page 80: Pythagorean Theorem

1. S=123.467

2. S=145.214

3. S=182.077

4. S=190.394

5. S=77.104

6. S=100.583

7. S=61.164

8. S=55.642

9. S=90.067

10. S=74.733

11. S=43.715

12. S=107.926

13. S=158.294

14. S=162.610

15. S=114.769

16. S=110.639

17. S=58.915

18. S=145.619

19. S=47.508

20. S=143.248